GALATIANS

FREEDOM IN CHRIST

Study by Mark Olson
Commentary by Burt Burleson

Free downloadable Teaching Guide for this study available at
NextSunday.com/teachingguides

NextSunday Resources
6316 Peake Road
Macon, Georgia 31210-3960
1-800-747-3016
©2009 by NextSunday Resources
All rights reserved.
Printed in the United States of America.

The paper used in this publication meets the minimum requirements of
American National Standard for Information Sciences—
Permanence of Paper for Printed Library Materials.
ANSI Z39.48–1984. (alk. paper)

Library of Congress Cataloging-in-Publication Data

CIP Information on file.

TABLE OF CONTENTS

Galatians: Freedom in Christ

HOW TO USE THIS STUDY

NextSunday Resources Adult Bible Studies are designed to help adults study Scripture seriously within the context of the larger Christian tradition and, through that process, find their faith renewed, challenged, and strengthened. We study the Scriptures because we believe they affect our current lives in important ways. Each study contains the following three components:

Study Guide

Each study guide lesson is arranged in five movements:

Reflecting recalls a contemporary story, anecdote, example, or illustration to help us anticipate the session's relevance in our lives.

Remembering provides a frame of reference for the Scriptures.

Studying is centered on giving the biblical material in-depth attention while often surrounding it with helpful insights from theology, ethics, church history, and other areas.

Understanding helps us find relevant connections between our lives and the biblical message.

What About Me? provides brief statements that help unite life issues with the meaning of the biblical text.

Commentary

Each study guide lesson is accompanied by an additional, in-depth commentary on the biblical material. Written by a different author than the study guide, each commentary gives the opportunity for learners to approach the Scripture text from a separate but complementary viewpoint.

Teaching Guide

In addition to the provided study guide and commentary, *NextSunday Resources* also provides a *free* downloadable teaching guide, available at NextSunday.com. Each teaching guide gives the teacher tools for focusing on the content of each study guide lesson through additional commentary and Bible background information. Through teacher helps and teaching options, each teaching guide also provides substance for variety and choice in the preparation of each lesson.

NextSunday
Resources

STUDY INTRODUCTION

These five lessons cover almost the entire letter that Paul wrote to the Christians living in Galatia, an area of the Roman Empire in central Asia Minor, during the late forties AD. It was possibly the first written of all the "books" in the New Testament. Paul wrote with fiery passion, as you will notice in the opening paragraphs of this letter. His language may even shock you! But his language reveals that he was writing about a crucially important issue—the very nature of salvation in Christ.

Remember that Paul was born and raised as a devout Jew in the Gentile city of Tarsus and that he eventually became a Pharisee, a strict upholder of the Jewish law. Before his conversion on the road to Damascus, Paul tried to please God by obeying every detail of the Torah, the Jewish law detailed in the Old Testament. After meeting the risen Christ, Paul realized that God had provided a new way for both Jews and Gentiles to be justified. Because Jesus Christ, the Messiah, died on the cross, both Jews and Gentiles could be justified through faith in Christ. In fact, that was the only way that Jews and Gentiles could be justified!

In the first lesson, "Establishing Your Credentials," Paul reveals details about his personal life that clearly reveal that his calling to serve as an apostle came not through other apostles but from God alone. Lesson two, "Living Out What We Say We Believe," probes the issue of hypocrisy and asks each reader to consider how our lifestyle sometimes fails to reflect the theology we profess. The third lesson asks a question: "If God Gave the Law, Don't We All Have to Obey It?" This lesson explores the question that Paul certainly faced on numerous occasions, since the Old Testament makes it clear that God was the one who gave the law. Lesson four, "Set Free by Christ," connects Galatians to the twenty-first century. In our final lesson, "You Raise Me Up," we explore the ways in which Christians can help one another grow spiritually.

ESTABLISHING YOUR CREDENTIALS

Galatians 1

Central Question

How do we define our faith?

Scripture

Galatians 1 Paul an apostle—sent neither by human commission nor from human authorities, but through Jesus Christ and God the Father, who raised him from the dead— 2 and all the members of God's family who are with me, To the churches of Galatia: 3 Grace to you and peace from God our Father and the Lord Jesus Christ, 4 who gave himself for our sins to set us free from the present evil age, according to the will of our God and Father, 5 to whom be the glory forever and ever. Amen. 6 I am astonished that you are so quickly deserting the one who called you in the grace of Christ and are turning to a different gospel— 7 not that there is another gospel, but there are some who are confusing you and want to pervert the gospel of Christ. 8 But even if we or an angel from heaven should proclaim to you a gospel contrary to what we proclaimed to you, let that one be accursed! 9 As we have said before, so now I repeat, if anyone proclaims to you a gospel contrary to what you received, let that one be accursed! 10 Am I now seeking human approval, or God's approval? Or am I trying to please people? If I were still pleasing people, I would not be a servant of Christ. 11 For I want you to know, brothers and sisters, that the gospel that was proclaimed by me is not of human origin; 12 for I did not receive it from a human source, nor was I taught it, but I received it through a revelation of Jesus Christ. 13 You have heard, no doubt, of my earlier life in Judaism. I was violently persecuting the church of God and was trying to destroy it. 14 I advanced in Judaism beyond many among my people of the same age, for I was far more zealous for the traditions of my ancestors. 15 But when God, who had set me apart before I was born and called me through his grace, was pleased 16 to reveal his Son to me, so that I might proclaim him among the Gentiles, I did not confer with any human being, 17 nor did I go up to Jerusalem to those who were already apostles before me, but I went away at once into Arabia, and afterwards I returned to Damascus. 18 Then after three years I did go up to Jerusalem to visit Cephas and stayed with him fifteen days; 19 but I did not see any other apostle except James the Lord's brother. 20 In what I am writing to you, before God, I do not lie! 21 Then I went into the regions of Syria and Cilicia, 22 and I was still unknown by sight to the churches of Judea that are in Christ; 23 they only heard it said, "The one who formerly was persecuting us is now proclaiming the faith he once tried to destroy." 24 And they glorified God because of me.

Reflecting

During any presidential election season, both major candidates typically reveal significant portions of their personal histories in autobiographical works. Often they must respond to events that portray them in a negative light, at least for some observers. However, each also seeks to tell their stories in ways that might allow the typical American to interpret these events as part of a broader story with a positive outcome.

Consider how Paul faced a similar dilemma to our presidential candidates. Many people knew he had once persecuted the church and helped execute the early Christian preacher Stephen. How could he admit that terrible sin and still convince his readers to believe his interpretation of the Christian faith? How could he bare his soul and, at the same time, establish his credentials as a true apostle of Jesus Christ?

Remembering

For centuries, Protestant Christians have taken for granted the spiritual motto, "People are saved by faith, not works." For many, it is difficult to imagine a Christianity that is based on anything other than this premise. However, it was once hotly debated. Opponents not only challenged this version of Christianity, but also the personal motives of its leading supporter. Intimidated, previous supporters began to waffle. In addition, loud missionaries preached a different version of Christianity that was gaining popularity. Paul stood alone.

This month, we'll explore this volatile situation in the province of Galatia, part of the Roman Empire. Paul, the church-planting missionary, struggled to keep his newly established churches from switching to a version of Christianity that was markedly different from the one he taught. We will strive to understand the crisis he faced and the issues that drove him to write a letter that amounted to a verbal blitzkrieg against his opponents. We'll sense his anger. Finally, we'll come to understand this man from Tarsus more completely and appreciate how crucial his contribution to our faith is.

Paul established the first churches in Galatia on his first mission trip, which included stops in Iconium, Lystra, and Derbe (see Acts 13:14–14:23). On his second and third mission trips, he traveled through the northern part of Galatia (near modern-day Ankara), where he may have started churches as well. Under Paul's preaching and teaching, these churches flourished, and a significant number of people accepted Christ as Lord and Savior. Though Paul was a Jewish Christian and probably brought some Jewish

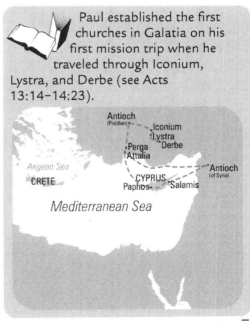

Paul established the first churches in Galatia on his first mission trip when he traveled through Iconium, Lystra, and Derbe (see Acts 13:14–14:23).

Antioch
(Pisidian)
Iconium
Lystra
Perga   Derbe
Attalia
Aegean Sea
CRETE   CYPRUS
Paphos   Salamis
Antioch
(of Syria)

Mediterranean Sea

Christians into these churches, he focused on winning Gentiles to faith in Christ.

Later, Paul learned that some of the Galatian churches were dividing over the preaching of other Jewish-Christian missionaries who taught *a different gospel* from the one Paul preached. They taught that faith in Christ was not sufficient; to be a full believer, one had to obey the most important aspects of the Jewish law—circumcision, food laws, and Sabbath observances. Since Paul could not debate these new missionaries in person, he wrote a fiery letter to convince the Galatian Christians that faith in Christ was all they needed for salvation.

Studying

We read Paul's first words to the Galatians, "Paul, an apostle," and question, "Well, didn't everyone know Paul was an apostle?" Many early Christians reserved the term "apostle" for the original twelve disciples. By that definition of "apostle," Paul was not qualified. He was not one of the Twelve, nor was he even an assistant to Peter, John, or one of the others. Regardless, Paul boldly claimed the title "apostle." He further states that his commission was directly from Jesus Christ and from the One who raised Jesus Christ from the dead. His comments hint at the event that led directly to his calling—the resurrection.

Matthias, who replaced Judas in Acts 1:26, was also considered an apostle.

In most of his letters, Paul begins by praising his readers for some positive spiritual accomplishment, but in Galatians, he moves right from his greeting to a personal attack: "I am astonished that you are so quickly deserting the one who called you into the grace of Christ and are turning to a different gospel" (v. 6). He was severely disappointed that the new missionaries had so strongly influenced the Galatian Christians. Furthermore, he was furious with the Jewish-Christian missionaries themselves. In fact, Paul was so angry that he directed a curse at them for perverting the basic Christian message (vv. 8-9)!

Apparently, these missionaries (some scholars call them "Judaizers") agreed with Paul that Gentiles and Jews should believe in Jesus as the Messiah. However, they added requirements for salvation, teaching that all believers in Christ must at least follow the key tenets of the Old Testament Torah: circumcision, food laws, and Sabbath observances. More specifically, that meant Gentile Christians had to rest on Saturday and eliminate pork from their diet, and that the males had to undergo adult circumcision. These Judaizers told the Galatians that Paul had watered down the requirements to become a Christian and they were going to correct this shortcoming. They, unlike Paul, were giving the full requirements for salvation. Furthermore, the Galatians could trust these new missionaries because their message came from leaders in the original Jerusalem church—true apostles, people who really knew Jesus Christ in the flesh.

Paul responded by insisting that his gospel (which means "good news") came from a higher source than a mere human being; it came from Jesus Christ himself (v. 12). He then established his credentials by bearing his soul to his Galatian Christian readers. He gave his version of the events from Acts 7–9 (the stoning of Stephen and journey to Damascus). He admitted that before his conversion to Christianity he violently persecuted the church and tried to destroy it. Then God revealed Jesus to Paul and called Paul to preach the message about Christ to the Gentiles.

Paul offers additional details of his life after conversion, but not from a selfish desire to present his own spiritual résumé. He wanted only to prove that he received the gospel message directly from Christ, *not* first from any of the twelve apostles. That is why he so adamantly insists that, following his conversion, "I did not confer with any human being, nor did I go up to Jerusalem to those who were apostles before me" (vv. 16-17). Only after he had been preaching the gospel for three years did Paul finally meet two of the apostles—Cephas (Peter) and James the brother of Jesus. Even then, he only spent fifteen days with Peter and apparently less time with James. Other

Acts alone tells us that Paul's conversion event happened on the road to Damascus.

members of churches in Judea did not even know Paul by sight (v. 22). Paul includes these statements to demonstrate that he was not an assistant to the original twelve apostles who had somehow watered down their full gospel message, which apparently was what his opponents in Galatia were saying. Plus, they said he was a liar (v. 20)!

Paul counters his opponents by demonstrating that his commission to take the message of Christ to the Gentiles came from Christ himself, no one else. In Galatians 2–6, he elaborates on that basic gospel message, but in chapter 1, Paul builds his case squarely on his experience of the resurrection.

Understanding

Most of us like to think ourselves open-minded. We pride ourselves on our civility toward those with different perspectives from our own. How do we react to Paul calling down a curse on his opponents? Actually, he was so angry that he pronounced the curse twice (vv. 8-9)!

Are there any issues so important that we cannot afford to allow different perspectives to stand without challenging them? Paul sometimes demonstrated wide tolerance for different perspectives on religious issues (see his views on the appropriate day to worship in Romans 14:5-6). However, in Galatians 1, Paul's personal testimony makes it clear that it is intolerable for Christians to change the requirements for salvation.

What about your personal testimony? Are there events in your life that you would be reluctant to admit? Would it one day be possible for God to weave these events into a larger historical tapestry of your life in a way that honored God? After his conversion, Paul was surely ashamed of his role in Stephen's murder. But, eventually, God showed him how to make that shameful event part of a testimony of God's grace to Paul. Let God do the same in your life.

What issues do you consider essential to the Christian faith?

What About Me?

• *How can you "bare your soul" in a way that reveals God's grace in your life?* Are you able to tell your spiritual story to nonbelievers in a way that encourages them to talk more about what God could do in their lives? Using Paul as your model, can you share your testimony to encourage others who have shared your failings?

• *The resurrection of Jesus Christ included both his ascent from the tomb and his appearance to several people.* Paul was the last person to whom the risen Christ appeared. That resurrection appearance drastically changed Paul's life and dramatically shifted the direction of the early church.

• *Many issues churches face need more tolerance and effort toward understanding diverse viewpoints from all members.* Choose wisely where you are going to dig in your heels and refuse to budge. Paul stood firm on the con-ditions of salvation. He considered them essential to the Christian gospel. Know what is essential for the Christian faith, and take your stand alongside Paul.

Resources

James L. Blevins, "Opponents of Paul," *The Mercer Dictionary of the Bible*, ed. Watson E. Mills et al. (Macon GA: Mercer University Press, 1990).

F. F. Bruce, *Commentary on Galatians*, New International Greek Testament Commentary (Grand Rapids MI: Eerdmans, 1982).

Richard N. Longenecker, *Galatians*, Word Biblical Commentary (Dallas: Word, 1990).

Mark J. Olson, *Galatians: In Defense of Love* (Macon GA: Smyth & Helwys Publishing, 1994).

ESTABLISHING
YOUR CREDENTIALS

Galatians 1

Introduction

As you study Galatians, there are two ideas to keep in mind throughout the study. One is the question: Who is being transformed? The other is Paul's bottom line, which is that God is making of the believer a new creation. Everything else pales in comparison: *"Neither circumcision nor uncircumcision really matters...all that matters is a new creation"* (6:15).

First, let's explore the question: Who is being transformed? The question comes in response to a controversy in the Galatian church. The Jewish Christians, who loved their religion and Jesus, wanted the non-Jewish Christians to love their religion too—and practice it. In fact, they went so far as to insist that practicing it was necessary for salvation.

When people came forward at the end of the worship service in response to the invitation to be a follower of Christ, they were ushered into the counseling room, which also doubled as a clinic for circumcision. Plenty of folks in this new movement were supportive of this practice. And why not? Jesus was a practicing Jew, as were all the apostles. God had chosen the Jews as special recipients of God's disclosure, not only through the law, but now also through Jesus. It was natural to view Christ as an extension of what God had done previously through the law. Christianity was a new and improved Judaism with Jesus as the best and brightest interpreter of the Scriptures.

Before we cast twenty-first-century stones at "those closed-minded first-century believers," slow down and think about how much you value your own traditions. They matter, don't they?

They've been vehicles for God's revelation to you, facilitators of your experience with the Divine. Traditions matter.

Even more importantly, The Tradition, their heritage as God's chosen people, the law and how they have understood it, matters. That is ultimately what was at stake for the Galatians. This issue wasn't as simple as, *"We've never done it that way before."* This question is about God's revelation, how the church received it, and how the church would pass it on. Paul was asking the Galatians to let go of The Tradition...revealed...understood...and even validated by many who were followers of Jesus.

I. Making the Case

This background brings us to the first chapter. Paul needed to make a case for his authority to take these good, God-fearing, Jesus-following people away from The Tradition. Such a change is one that most of us would struggle with, if not resist with all our being. If, for example, a charismatic soul showed up in church one Sunday and asked us to do away with the Lord's Supper, we would likely say, "Not on your life. This ordinance has been revealed and passed down to us. You'll need to show us your credentials to even get a good hearing."

Paul is showing his credentials in chapter 1. He understood what was at stake and had obviously received word that some Galatians were questioning his authority to take them down this new, seemingly "heretical" road. These "Judaizers" reminded folks, "Remember, Paul wasn't one of the Twelve. He wasn't actually with Jesus. Jesus said he wasn't coming to do away with the law, and he certainly never advised foregoing circumcision. You can't find that in the Scriptures. Paul's an impressive guy, but we dare not forget Moses."

Paul had heard the Judaizers' arguments, so he begins his letter with bold words: "Paul, an apostle," which means, "one sent." Paul wanted to make sure from the beginning that the Galatians remembered he wasn't sent from men. God, through Jesus, sent Paul.

II. The Question of Authority

It's important to note that while Paul was bucking the tradition-alists, he was not advocating an "authority-less" community. Today, we are uncomfortable with authority, especially as we've seen it wielded in such immature and un-Christlike ways. We are even tempted to punt the notion that God places people among us to lead us.

Paul says, "I'm an apostle...listen to me." Certainly, such a claim comes with a corresponding vulnerability to be corrupted by arrogance and narcissism; however, that reality did not keep Paul from being bold.

Paul's model for authority was Jesus. Jesus taught what he knew to be true as one "sent by God." He eventually called his disciples "friends" because they had come to know everything Jesus knew (see John's Gospel). However, Paul recognizes that now is the time for teaching and for learning.

Consider whether there is anyone in your life you've trusted to be your teacher, someone with whom you suspend all your suspicion and your need to be in charge and in control. Americans don't find it easy to submit to authority. We sing "I Did It My Way," claim the priesthood of the believer, and think ourselves progressive. This bold individualism is not the way to a new creation, which is the point of Paul's letter. There's a journey to be made to real freedom. There is much to learn on our way to that transformed destination. Authority has a place.

III. Authority in Christ

Paul boldly claimed his authority based on his experience with Christ. Nowhere does Paul say that for all time and in all places, rituals and traditions don't matter. He did not advocate abolishing the Galatians' Tradition. He simply says that the Spirit and individual experience matter. God's spirit acted in a specific way in Paul's life. God opened his eyes and gave him good news to preach. We can understand Paul's perspective because we believe that sometimes God breaks through and gives us a new word. We know God works in powerful ways through people. So when Paul makes this very personal claim based upon his transforming experience with God, we're open to it. Tradition is a dynamic reality, and the spirit of God has a way of trumping it from time to time.

Paul's gifts of self-confidence, clarity, and passion were destined (v. 15) and needed for that time. Paul, in light of his own experience of transformation, came to see the heart of Jesus' teachings as a movement beyond the legalism so prominent in that day. He brings a new and transforming word about God's past revelation.

God's mercy is a gift—period. There is nothing to do, nothing to be done on our part. It's grace. We belong to God because God wants it that way. We can't escape it, nor can we create it. All we can do is be open to receiving it.

This theology is so familiar to us. We've heard it preached a million times. But remember, as you work through Galatians this month, that God used Paul to insist upon it in the new movement called Christianity.

IV. Authority Understood and Shared in Community

Paul wasn't the only one preaching this new message. A teacher of mine says that God doesn't play "peek-a-boo" with us. Revelation isn't dependent upon one moment or one person. While God used Paul, this teaching was not unique to Paul, and he says as much in the first sentence: "and all the brothers with me," meaning Paul was working out of a community, a local church. Paul was in conversation with believers, and as we know from Acts, one of his good friends disagreed with him at times (see Barnabas).

Paul also says in verse 17 that he spent three years in Damascus following some time alone in the desert. This time alone and in Damascus shaped his theology. He eventually met with Peter, at time when he listened and learned. So it's apparent in chapter 1 that, bold as Paul was, he wasn't an apostolic Lone Ranger.

It is also clear that God was making known this inclusive, expanded notion of grace in other places. Peter's vision in Acts 10 is a good example of this revelation. In addition, and most importantly, Jesus himself taught the expansion of God's grace to everyone.

Paul's message surely wasn't his alone. In addition to other apostles whose hearts were opened to the Gentiles knowing God apart from their religion, and in addition to Jesus' gracious ways, there were people in the Galatian church who knew at a deep level that salvation in Christ wasn't about circumcision. God was making of them new creations. They could not deny it (see 3:2). They knew Paul's understanding of the gospel was right because they were experiencing it.

Of course, Paul's letter to the Galatians did not close the case, and those prone to legalism ducked away in defeat. Deciding what is right in the context of community takes time. Traditions matter...The Tradition matters...Scripture matters...as do those prophetic voices that seem to run counter to what we've known. However, we must remember that one person with a minority opinion wrote half of our New Testament. Centuries later, we consider his minority opinion the word of the Lord. Thanks be to God.

Notes

Notes

LIVING OUT WHAT
WE SAY WE BELIEVE

Galatians 2

Central Question

How should we live if we believe that we are "justified by faith"?

Scripture

Galatians 2 Then after fourteen years I went up again to Jerusalem with Barnabas, taking Titus along with me. 2 I went up in response to a revelation. Then I laid before them (though only in a private meeting with the acknowledged leaders) the gospel that I proclaim among the Gentiles, in order to make sure that I was not running, or had not run, in vain. 3 But even Titus, who was with me, was not compelled to be circumcised, though he was a Greek. 4 But because of false believers secretly brought in, who slipped in to spy on the freedom we have in Christ Jesus, so that they might enslave us— 5 we did not submit to them even for a moment, so that the truth of the gospel might always remain with you. 6 And from those who were supposed to be acknowledged leaders (what they actually were makes no difference to me; God shows no partiality)—those leaders contributed nothing to me. 7 On the contrary, when they saw that I had been entrusted with the gospel for the uncircumcised, just as Peter had been entrusted with the gospel for the circumcised 8 (for he who worked through Peter making him an apostle to the circumcised also worked through me in sending me to the Gentiles), 9 and when James and Cephas and John, who were acknowledged pillars, recognized the grace that had been given to me, they gave to Barnabas and me the right hand of fellowship, agreeing that we should go to the Gentiles and they to the circumcised. 10 They asked only one thing, that we remember the poor, which was actually what I was eager to do. 11 But when Cephas came to Antioch, I opposed him to his face, because he stood self-condemned; 12 for until certain people came from James, he used to eat with the Gentiles. But after they came, he drew back and kept himself separate for fear of the circumcision faction. 13 And the other Jews joined him in this hypocrisy, so that even Barnabas was led astray by their hypocrisy. 14 But when I saw that they were not acting consistently with the truth of the gospel, I said to Cephas before them all, "If you, though a Jew, live like a Gentile and not like a Jew, how can you compel the Gentiles to live like Jews?" 15 We ourselves are Jews by birth and not Gentile sinners; 16 yet we know that a person is justified not by the works of the law but through faith in Jesus Christ. And we have come to believe in Christ Jesus, so that we might be justified by faith in Christ, and not by doing the works of the law, because no one will be justified by the works of the law. 17 But if, in our effort to be justified in Christ, we ourselves have been found to be sinners, is Christ then a servant of sin? Certainly not! 18 But if I build up again the very things that I once tore down, then I demonstrate that I am a transgressor. 19 For through the law I died to the law, so that I might live to God. I have been crucified with Christ; 20 and it is no longer I who live, but it is Christ who lives in me. And the life I now live in the flesh I live by faith in the Son of God, who loved me and gave himself for me. 21 I do not nullify the grace of God; for if justification comes through the law, then Christ died for nothing.

Reflecting

In the 1967 movie *Guess Who's Coming to Dinner?*, Spencer Tracy and Katharine Hepburn play an upper-middle-class couple, Matt and Christina Drayton, who say they believe in racial equality, but suddenly have to decide how much they really believe their own words. Their daughter, Joey, returns from a Hawaiian vacation announcing that she wants to marry a brilliant research physician, John Prentice. It's every parent's dream—except that

John is black. Matt and Christina struggle to reconcile the moral values they say they believe with the real possibility of social ostracism from their circle of friends.

Most adult Christians who have followed Christ for a decade or two are fairly clear about the basic doctrines they say they believe. However, this week's session highlights a difficult situation in the first century that caused many leading Christians, including Peter, to act in ways inconsistent with the faith they proclaimed. At times, all of us are tempted to betray our faith by acting hypocritically. Only if we admit this possibility can we truly appreciate the depth of the crisis caused by the hypocrisy and the heroic stand that overcame the crisis.

Remembering

Last week, we reviewed Paul's founding of the churches in Galatia during his missionary journeys and learned how Jewish-Christian missionaries who delivered a very different gospel from the one Paul preached had invaded these churches. They taught that all Christians needed to follow the Old Testament law, especially the regulations concerning circumcision, food, and Sabbath. Paul countered by writing this fiery letter to the Galatian believers to win them back to the true gospel.

The longest autobiographical sketch in any New Testament writing is found in 1:11-21. Paul wrote this not for self-promotion, but to establish his credentials as a true apostle. The Jewish-Christian missionaries (also known as Judaizers) so forcibly attacked Paul's credentials that he had to defend his own credibility to congregations that he had established! He did so by pointing out that his calling as an apostle came not from a mere human being, but from the resurrected Christ himself! Christ also gave Paul the commission to take the Christian message to the Gentiles.

Paul paid special attention to Jerusalem in his autobiographical sketch because it was the center of Jewish Christianity. Not all Jewish Christians were Judaizers; after all, Paul continued to consider himself both Jewish and Christian. But Judaizers did claim their authority from some of the apostles in Jerusalem.

Therefore, Paul took special care to prove his independence from Jerusalem and from the apostles who ministered there. If the Judaizers could show that Paul was a minor league assistant to the real apostles in Jerusalem, then they could argue that whatever Peter or James said was more authoritative than anything Paul had to say. They could claim that they, the Judaizers, were "correcting" Paul based on what they had heard the "real" apostles say. Paul refused to allow them to make this argument. In chapter 1, he demonstrates that his apostleship came directly from the risen Christ, not from any of the Jerusalem apostles. Furthermore, after his conversion, he preached the gospel for three years before he ever went to Jerusalem. Now, in chapter 2, he finishes his autobiographical sketch and concludes with one of the strongest statements of the basic gospel message of the entire New Testament.

Studying

Scholars who try to reconstruct the chronology of the early church love the book of Acts and this autobiographical section in Galatians because they give some details. However, even these details are not as precise as they first seem. For example, Paul says in 2:1 that they went up to Jerusalem "after 14 years." But does he mean fourteen years after his conversion on the road to Damascus or fourteen years after his first visit to Jerusalem? Scholars are divided in their interpretation. Fortunately, Paul's major purpose is not to give an exact chronology, but to establish his independence from and equality with the apostles in Jerusalem.

Knowing that controversial events must be recounted fairly, Paul let his readers know that Barnabas and Titus, who were eyewitnesses, could confirm the details of this second Jerusalem visit (2:1). By this time, Paul was a veteran missionary and experienced preacher and debater. He needed all the skills and confidence he had developed to negotiate the

Note that this James is the brother of Jesus, not James the son of Zebedee and brother of John. That James had already been executed by King Herod, as recounted in Acts 12:2.

crucial events that took place in Jerusalem. Knowing that his mission to take the gospel to the Gentiles was controversial with some in Jerusalem, Paul met privately with the leaders of the Jerusalem church. Apparently, some Judaizers slipped in secretly and tried to challenge the validity of Paul's mission (2:4-5). But the leaders of the Jerusalem church—including the key apostles James, Cephas (Peter), and John—recognized that God was accomplishing great things through Paul, and they affirmed his entire ministry to the Gentiles (2:9). They did not do this reluctantly or with misgivings; rather, they gave Paul and Barnabas "the right hand of fellowship"—a complete affirmation. They decided that while they would continue to preach the gospel to Jews, Paul and Barnabas could continue to preach the gospel to Gentiles. The only request they made of Paul was that he remember the poor, a request he honored later in his ministry by undertaking the first large-scale mission offering in Christian history and delivering the money to the poor in Jerusalem. They did not request that he modify his message in any way. They even accepted Titus, an uncircumcised Gentile Christian, as a fellow believer (2:3). This meeting was a total victory for Paul. However, the battle for full inclusion of Gentile Christians was not over.

See 1 Cor 16:1-3; 2 Cor 8:1-15; Rom 15:25-29.

Paul tells the Galatian readers about one more event that illuminates his role in allowing Gentiles to come to faith in Christ without following the Jewish law. This event took place in Antioch, within the congregation that first sent Paul out on his missionary journeys. It is an amazing testimony to the truthfulness of Scripture that this event is recorded in the Bible because it paints two of the most important early Christian leaders, Peter and James, in a bad light.

Paul explains that Peter came to Antioch and affirmed the Gentile Christians there by joining them for meals. That may not seem like much to us, but remember that strict Jews did not eat meals with Gentiles because Gentiles ate food disallowed by the Old Testament—foods like pork and shellfish. Acts 10:10-35 tells how God spoke to Peter in a dream and told him that he could now eat foods previously considered unclean. Peter followed up on this new insight by sharing meals with new Gentile-Christian converts and treating them as equals.

Today we would say that these Gentiles ate foods that were not kosher.

Then, "certain people came from James" (2:12) and began pressuring the Jewish Christians, like Peter, to stop sharing meals with Gentiles, even though these Gentiles were believers in Christ. Whether or not these newcomers honestly represented James's sentiments, we don't know. But they spoke with enough authority that Peter (called by his Aramaic name Cephas) completely caved in. So did Barnabas, Paul's fellow missionary to the Gentiles (2:13).

The entire Christian movement was in grave danger. If Paul had not stood firm at this moment, if he had given in to the Judaizers and refused to eat with Gentile Christians, the mission to the Gentiles might have collapsed. How many Romans and Greeks would have joined a church led by Jewish Christians who treated them like second-class believers? How many would have found genuine fellowship with people who told them, "Yes, Jesus died for you, but I'm not going to eat lunch with you!" Paul's bold stand likely saved the Christian movement from disaster.

Paul points out that Peter and Barnabas were not living out the faith they professed. They were acting hypocritically. He demanded that their actions match their theology.

Our word "hypocrite" comes from the Greek word *hupokrinomai* in 2:13.

In his most famous letter to the Romans, Paul begins with theology (chs. 1–11) and then moves to ethics (chs. 12–15). In Galatians, he begins with ethics (should Jewish Christians share a meal with Gentile Christians?) and then moves to theology. His theological understanding is brilliant! He begins by affirming that he is still Jewish (2:15), but then insists that obeying the Jewish law justifies no one. Only by coming to faith in Jesus Christ are we justified (2:16). His Galatian readers already believed in Jesus, so they were already full Christians.

Understanding

Paul points out that the terrible event of Christ's crucifixion only makes sense if it delivers all believers from spiritual death. Only if a great victory is won, and Jews and Gentiles alike gain access to salvation through faith in the crucified one...only then can we understand why God allowed Jesus to die such an agonizing death. Paul explains that those who insisted that Gentiles had to follow the Old Testament law were nullifying the cross of Christ: "If justification comes through the law, then Christ died for nothing" (2:21). Only a Christianity that welcomes all people on the basis of faith alone, not works of the law, makes sense of the crucifixion.

Most of us will affirm that we are justified, or saved, by faith in Jesus Christ. However, do we always live out our theology? When we worship only with people similar to us, we imply that Christ's death was somehow not quite good enough to fully save all people. When we eat all of our meals with people of the same socioeconomic status, we send a message to other believers (whether they be richer or poorer than we are) that Christ's death did not quite bridge the economic gap. As Peter and Barnabas discovered, it really is hard to live out one's faith consistently. Paul insists, however, that we do it!

What About Me?

• *If you believe that all people can be justified, or saved, by faith in Jesus Christ, what changes do you or your congregation need to make to live that faith out more consistently?* How can you treat all believers as full recipients of God's grace?

• *Can you imagine what the Christian faith would have become if Paul had backed down and lost this argument with the Judaizers?* How many Gentiles in the Roman world would have come to faith in Christ if they were treated as second-class believers, unworthy of sharing a meal with the Jewish Christians who worshiped with them? Would you be willing to be a member of a church that consistently treated you as a second-class member?

• *Paul demonstrates what a tremendous impact one believer can have if he or she stands firmly on the basic truth of the Christian faith.* Even if others around you sometimes live hypocritically, let Paul's courageous example inspire you to speak boldly for your faith.

Resources

Richard N. Longenecker, *Galatians*, Word Biblical Commentary (Dallas: Word, 1990).

Scott McKnight, *Galatians*, The NIV Application Commentary (Grand Rapids MI: Zondervan, 1995).

Mark J. Olson, *Galatians: In Defense of Love* (Macon GA: Smyth & Helwys Publishing, 1994).

LIVING OUT WHAT
WE SAY WE BELIEVE

Galatians 2

Introduction

One thing is clear in Galatians 2: Confessing faith in Christ doesn't automatically remove the brokenness in our lives. Often, we live out of that brokenness rather than from Christlikeness. We have what one writer calls "an operational theology" (Merle Jordan, *Taking on the Gods* [Nashville: Abingdon Press, 1986], 87). It's that theology down in the gut that drives who we are Monday through Friday. It's the theology that those who know us best experience in us daily. It's deeper than the doctrine in our heads. It isn't "confessed with our mouths" but rather with our behavior and attitudes.

Old habits die hard, and embedded doctrines don't die—they linger. Unless, that is, we are willing to identify and let go of them and sometimes even battle against them.

I. Making a New Creation

Remember, the entire letter to the Galatians is moving toward the conclusion that God is making of us a new creation. God's new creation begins in an initial "knowing" or understanding of God's great love and grace. It is sometimes a miraculous change in someone's life and, at the least, an initial "break" with old ways of living. However, as we've all experienced, the old ways often return.

Peter is a good example of our human tendency to return to old ways and old theology. God had shown Peter something new: God's grace was for everyone (Acts 10). Peter had opened his heart to Gentile believers and celebrated their faith in Christ. He cham-pioned their inclusion into the church. That was his theology.

However, something of Peter's old theology lingered, and there came a day when Peter wouldn't sit with the Gentiles in the church at meals. Something under the surface of God's new creation got the best of him. He took his plate and sat with his old crowd, isolating the Gentiles and proclaiming with his behavior that God's love for them wasn't enough. His actions conveyed that the Gentiles were second-class citizens in the kingdom and that they could contaminate him by their presence.

II. The Early Church—A Work in Progress

Galatians 2 reiterates the teachings of chapter 1 because some folks in church were adding to the gospel (and, thereby, the freedom found in Christ) by interpreting that Christians had to adhere to a legal code as well. This debate was ongoing in the early church. Early Christians were still working out what they'd heard, seen, and experienced in Jesus, and it was not an easy task. They had to make sense of and articulate what God had revealed through Jesus. God had begun the work in Jesus, but the church was left with some work to do as well.

God seems to prefer this cooperative way of creating. In Genesis, God created the animals, and Adam named them. God gets things started and then invites us to join the process. We always have a part to play.

The morning after the resurrection, the disciples weren't sitting about discussing the doctrine of the Trinity. Jesus was alive, raised from the dead! The implications of that event took some time to articulate. They had not begun to understand it all. Eventually, after plenty of conversation, the church said, "We don't comprehend this mystery, but we believe Jesus Christ was God in the flesh."

The earliest Christians were also "in conversation" about what to do with Judaism—this faith that was central to their lives *and* to their understanding of Jesus. Jesus was a practicing Jew, and while he clearly treated everyone equally worthy of his blessing, he didn't spell out what to do with the religion of his childhood. He left that significant work to the church.

III. Learning to Expand the Boundaries

As the church hammered out what they believed, they often hammered one another in the process. Truthfully, we have a tendency to go overboard with the interpretive task into which God has invited us. God calls us to think and articulate according to the revelation of God's spirit—the truth as we've experienced, studied, and known it. However, our tendency is to become carried away, trying to isolate ourselves from what is different. Because of sin, we are helplessly rooted in a self-centered or (at best) group-centered outlook of the world. We're egocentric and ethnocentric. We see ourselves and our tribe at the center and view the rest of the world from our perspective. What's more, we often feel it's our duty to force that perspective on the rest of the world.

The Galatian Christians had heard the good news that God's grace was theirs for the receiving. However, some Jewish evangelists were now saying, "You folks apparently haven't read the fine print of this New Covenant." This "fine print," of course, nullified the very gospel they'd received, but new Christians were vulnerable to following the old rules. They were making appointments for circumcision and starting to shop only at kosher markets. Even worse, they imagined God was pleased with them because of it.

Paul wrote this letter in an effort to rescue the Galatian Christians from any attempt to add fine print to a simple gospel that proclaims God's love as free to all who will receive it. Paul assured the Galatians that he understood how hard it is to let go of former beliefs and understandings. He reiterated, "This isn't easy. Even Simon Peter, the leader of the church in Jerusalem has struggled with these issues. At potluck, when some legalists were visiting, Peter caved and refused to sit with the Gentiles."

It's no surprise to us that Paul publicly confronted Peter (v. 14). Paul was not one to mince words or worry about someone's feelings, especially not with the gospel and his friends in Galatia at stake. However, Peter's spiritual health was also at stake. Paul confronted Peter, calling him to remember the gospel.

That is still one of the callings of the church. Lovingly and gently, we are to hold up mirrors for one another so that we can see the hypocrisies and inconsistencies of our lives. Perhaps Paul's model of public confrontation is not the best one to imitate; however, neither should we neglect confrontation for the sake of the gospel.

While we might question his means, we must affirm how Paul dealt with Peter. We don't know how the story ended, but in my imagination, Paul and Peter talked privately later. Peter's description of his actions might relate to us all: "Of course, I know you're right Paul. I knew what I did was wrong, but it's so hard. My body still reacts when I sit with Gentiles. It's uncanny. Something inside me also seems to need others' approval. I don't even like the legalists, but I have this inner drive to please them." Paul's reply may have been similar to Romans 7:15: "I do not understand my own actions. For I do not do what I want, but I do the very thing I hate."

Peter isn't the only one who struggled to integrate deed and creed. Consider the doctrines we confess on Sundays that are overwhelmed the rest of the week by beliefs more internal, instinctive, and ingrained deep within us. Remember, Paul wrote of Peter's incongruence so that we, perhaps, might see and own up to ours.

Jesus was clearly a champion for the poor, but there's a gap between that confession and what our checkbook reveals we really care about. Jesus said, "Don't worry; trust me; be at peace," but there's a gap because we can't seem to let go of our need to be in control. We're grumpy, not peaceful. Jesus said, "Forgive; don't judge," but there's a gap because we harbor resentments. We critique folks constantly. We confess that it's all about grace, but there's a gap because we are too often driven by guilt. We see Jesus serving, but we seek to dominate.

IV. Learning to Live Out of Grace

Incongruence by its nature is hard to recognize. Paul pointed out Peter's incongruence, and I suspect Peter could have returned the favor. Still, Paul insists that becoming a new creation is our destiny. Part of our responsibility is to identify the inconsistencies and acknowledge that there is work to do, *not work to gain*

God's favor, but work to live completely *in* God's favor. The work is about believing in and living deeply from God's grace.

That's what Paul is working on at the end of chapter 2. His faith in Christ was not simply some cognitive assent about Jesus' identity or a doctrinal proposition. It was his way of being.

Faith in Christ is a reality in which we live. It's an orientation of life. That's why Paul says, "I am crucified with Christ" (v. 19). As followers of Jesus, we do more than agree with the doctrines of the church about Jesus. We must actually follow Jesus. Jesus teaches us and demonstrates for us the way of letting go, the way of surrender and emptying. We find new life by dying to the old. We are crucified with Christ so the life of Christ can be lived in us. When and as that happens, we come to resemble the new creation about which Paul writes. We don't worry about who we're sitting beside at potluck. Our family members and friends start experiencing the grace we've been confessing on Sunday. We don't find it so hard to forgive or to take a deep breath and be at peace. Doxology and praise happen more often than complaint, compassion more than critique. Eventually, we realize we've been made new, and living what we say we believe isn't so hard. Thanks be to God.

Notes

Notes

3

IF GOD GAVE THE LAW, DON'T WE ALL NEED TO OBEY IT?

Galatians 3:1-9, 15-29

Central Question

Why did God give the law?

Scripture

Galatians 3:1-9, 15-29   You foolish Galatians! Who has bewitched you? It was before your eyes that Jesus Christ was publicly exhibited as crucified! 2 The only thing I want to learn from you is this: Did you receive the Spirit by doing the works of the law or by believing what you heard? 3 Are you so foolish? Having started with the Spirit, are you now ending with the flesh? 4 Did you experience so much for nothing?—if it really was for nothing. 5 Well then, does God supply you with the Spirit and work miracles among you by your doing the works of the law, or by your believing what you heard? 6 Just as Abraham "believed God, and it was reckoned to him as righteousness," 7 so, you see, those who believe are the descendants of Abraham. 8 And the scripture, foreseeing that God would justify the Gentiles by faith, declared the gospel beforehand to Abraham, saying, "All the Gentiles shall be blessed in you." 9 For this reason, those who believe are blessed with Abraham who believed.... 15 Brothers and sisters, I give an example from daily life: once a person's will has been ratified, no one adds to it or annuls it. 16 Now the promises were made to Abraham and to his offspring; it does not say, "And to offsprings," as of many; but it says, "And to your offspring," that is, to one person, who is Christ. 17 My point is this: the law, which came four hundred thirty years later, does not annul a covenant previously ratified by God, so as to nullify the promise. 18 For if the inheritance comes from the law, it no longer comes from the promise; but God granted it to Abraham through the promise. 19 Why then the law? It was added because of transgressions, until the offspring would come to whom the promise had been made; and it was ordained through angels by a mediator. 20 Now a mediator involves more than one party; but God is one. 21 Is the law then opposed to the promises of God? Certainly not! For if a law had been given that could make alive, then righteousness would indeed come through the law. 22 But the scripture has imprisoned all things under the power of sin, so that what was promised through faith in Jesus Christ might be given to those who believe. 23 Now before faith came, we were imprisoned and guarded under the law until faith would be revealed. 24 Therefore the law was our disciplinarian until Christ came, so that we might be justified by faith. 25 But now that faith has come, we are no longer subject to a disciplinarian, 26 for in Christ Jesus you are all children of God through faith. 27 As many of you as were baptized into Christ have clothed yourselves with Christ. 28 There is no longer Jew or Greek, there is no longer slave or free, there is no longer male and female; for all of you are one in Christ Jesus. 29 And if you belong to Christ, then you are Abraham's offspring, heirs according to the promise.

Reflecting

One of Harrison Ford's most memorable roles came in the powerful movie *Witness*. Ford's character, John Book, a tough Philadelphia cop who leaves the anarchy, violence, and immorality of the big city and flees to the Amish country in Pennsylvania, protects a young Amish boy who is the lone witness to the murder of an undercover policeman. While trying to hide by living as one of the Amish, he is first repelled by their old-fashioned ways and incredibly strict adherence to seemingly irrelevant regulations. No guns, no bright colors, no television, no telephones...nothing modern! They are the perfect example of legalists. Their laws rule every aspect of their lives. But eventually he comes to see the positive side of this legalism. Each person knows his or her role in society. They all know which behaviors are acceptable and which ones are not. They may be deeply alienated from the larger American society, but they feel an equally deep sense of community with one another. This feeling is beautifully portrayed when the entire community voluntarily joins together to build a large barn for a newly married couple. Detective Book realizes that their adherence to these old laws has allowed the Amish to create a very appealing lifestyle.

Until you make an effort to understand the deep appeal that such law-based living can provide, you will not understand why anyone would become a legalist. The Galatians were seriously considering adopting the Jewish law as an essential element in their Christian faith. They must have seen something quite appealing about the law to think about taking this step. Paul understood because he had been the ultimate legalist before his conversion. In Galatians 3, he answers the most powerful question that his opponents, the Judaizers, could have asked: "If God gave the law, don't we all need to obey it?"

Remembering

Last week, we finished the autobiographical section of Galatians. Paul gave a thumbnail sketch of his life to demonstrate that his version of Christianity, his gospel, came directly from Jesus Christ. He was converted during a resurrection appearance of Jesus Christ, and Christ told him to preach to the Gentiles. The apostles did not teach Paul, so no one could say that he misunderstood them. When he did meet the apostles in Jerusalem, they accepted his basic mission of taking the gospel to the Gentiles and conceded that Gentile converts did not have to follow the Jewish laws concerning circumcision and food. Peter and Barnabas did waver due to pressure from some Judaizers, and they temporarily stopped eating with Gentile Christians. However, Paul boldly challenged their hypocrisy and demanded that they permit Gentile Christians to live free of the Old Testament law.

Following his autobiographical account, Paul concludes Galatians 2 with a magnificent theological summary. Both Jews and Gentiles are justified, or saved, by faith in Jesus Christ, not by works of the law. Works of the law justify no one. If the law had been enough to provide salvation, then the Messiah would not have had to die on the cross. To say that justification comes through the law rather than faith in Christ nullifies Christ's death.

> But when Cephas came to Antioch, I opposed him to his face, because he stood self-condemned; for until certain people came from James, he used to eat with the Gentiles. But after they came, he drew back and kept himself separate for fear of the circumcision faction. And the other Jews joined him in this hypocrisy, so that even Barnabas was led astray by their hypocrisy. But when I saw that they were not acting consistently with the truth of the gospel, I said to Cephas before them all, "If you, though a Jew, live like a Gentile and not like a Jew, how can you compel the Gentiles to live like Jews?" (Gal 2:11-14)

Studying

Unable to visit Galatia, Paul wrote this important letter. He had to explain his basic position and anticipate his opponents' objections to provide persuasive counterarguments to their claims. Only such a letter could possibly win the Galatians back to the true gospel.

One of the most obvious arguments the Judaizers made against Paul centered on Abraham, great ancestor of the Jewish people. After all, Abraham was the first to be circumcised as a symbol of the covenant God made with him. God told Abraham, "Every male among you shall be circumcised" (Gen 17:10). So for more than 1,000 years, the Jewish people had considered themselves children of Abraham and circumcised all their male children to signify that they were under the covenant. Even Jews who observed few other Old Testament laws still obeyed the law about circumcision. They reasoned, "If God gave the law, don't we all need to obey it?"

In Galatians 3, Paul sets out to answer that question. He begins by making three points that demonstrate the superiority of faith over law:

• First, he reminds the Galatians that they received the Holy Spirit when they came to faith in Christ, even though they were not obeying the Old Testament law (3:1-5). Their experience of receiving the Spirit was God's sign that God was pleased with them—circumcision or other works of the law were not required to win God's approval.

• Second, Paul shares a brilliant insight to the Genesis story. He points out that well before Abraham was circumcised, he received God's promise that Abraham would be the father of a great nation. Abraham believed that God would fulfill the promise. Because the as-yet-uncircumcised Abraham had faith, God justified him, or declared him righteous. Paul quotes the crucial verse, Genesis 15:6, to prove his point: Abraham "believed God and it was reckoned to him as righteousness." Thus, Paul demonstrates that Abraham was justified on the basis of his faith, not on the basis of his works of the law, namely circumcision.

> Now the LORD said to Abram, "Go from your country and your kindred and your father's house to the land that I will show you. I will make of you a great nation, and I will bless you, and make your name great, so that you will be a blessing. I will bless those who bless you, and the one who curses you I will curse; and in you all the families of the earth shall be blessed." (Gen 12:1-3)

• Paul's third argument is that God's covenant with Abraham preceded God's covenant with Moses. That is, the covenant of the promise, which was received on faith, preceded the covenant of law. Paul concludes, "My point is this; the law, which came four hundred thirty years later, does not annul a covenant previously ratified by God, so as to nullify the promise" (3:17).

Assuming his readers would find these three arguments compelling, Paul goes on to answer the question he assumed the Judaizers would ask next: "Why then the law?" (3:19). One can almost hear the Judaizers arguing: "OK, so Abraham did have faith centuries before Moses received the law on Mount Sinai, but God still gave the law! Why did God give the law if God did not want us to follow it?"

The core of Paul's argument begins in 3:19 and continues in 3:23-26.

Paul answers that question in the rest of the chapter. He says that God added the law because of transgressions, *until* the offspring was born toward whom all the promises point—Jesus Christ (3:19). In other words, God gave the law to guard the covenant people *until* the Messiah arrived. Paul then explains that the law was like a *paidagogos*—which the NRSV translates as a "disciplinarian" (3:24). The *paidagogos* was a household slave used by the ancient Greeks to take care of their preschoolers. He taught basic skills such as letters and manners, but when the children were ready for school the *paidagogos* took them to a real teacher. We have no exact equivalent in America, but perhaps a stern British nanny is the closest modern equivalent. Like a nanny, the *paidagogos* performed a necessary task, but one that was preparatory and temporary.

The meaning of Paul's illustration is clear. God gave the Old Testament law—it was necessary—but its purpose was fulfilled when the Messiah came. God's children had been turned over to the master-teacher, Jesus Christ, and had no need of returning to the supervision of the *paidagogos*. Those who believed in Jesus were no longer under the law.

Faith in Jesus Christ was such a world-changing event that it shattered any barriers that previously divided people. Paul rejoiced that all who received Christ in faith and were baptized were now children of Abraham, heirs according to the promise. That meant Gentiles were justified by faith in Christ, just as Jews were; slaves were justified by that same faith, as were free people; females were justified by faith, just as males were (3:28). Faith in Christ over-came these previously important distinctions.

What barriers do we place on God's salvation today?

Understanding

Our society's increasing immoral tendencies deeply trouble many Americans. We ask questions such as these: Don't we need more

Americans hearing and obeying the commandment, "Do not commit adultery"? Wouldn't our society improve morally if more folks heeded the call, "Do not bear false witness"? Of course it would. Paul would agree. However, he would quickly add that obedience to the law does not make a person a believer in Christ. It does not justify anyone. We are saved, or justified, by believing in Jesus Christ.

Paul believed that the coming of Jesus Christ changed everything. Once Christ came, all the old barriers that divided people could fall. People could be united through a faith in Christ that made their other differences fade into insignificance. The differences between Jews and Gentiles (such as circumcision, Sabbath, and food laws) were meaningless. There was neither Jew nor Greek. Slaves might still have to work for their masters, but they were the same in Christ's eyes as free people. Men and women were essentially the same by virtue of their faith in Christ. Faith in Christ united all believers and made them one.

Today, we sometimes let other allegiances displace the all-important distinction of faith in Christ. We feel a sense of unity with all those who cheer for the same college football or basketball team. All the women in our garden club receive a warm smile from us. We quickly call a new member of our rotary lodge "friend." When we are traveling, we quickly greet folks from our home state. None of this is bad. We should develop close ties with other people. Paul would remind us that our most important human tie is to all who are justified by faith in Jesus Christ.

What About Me?

• *Christians who profess faith in Jesus Christ receive the Holy Spirit.* The presence of the Holy Spirit in our lives is one of God's signs that we have been changed.

• *Abraham's faith in God's promise justified him.* That means Abraham is the father of all who believe, Gentiles as well as Jews.

• *The Ten Commandments and the other Old Testament laws played a very important role in God's plan of salvation.* The law prepared the way for Jesus Christ, who fulfilled the law.

• *We must treat all Christians as our brothers and sisters in the faith.* People of different ethnic heritage, race, educational background, gender, or socioeconomic class must still find us reaching out to them as siblings. The coming of Christ has made us one. Our actions need to reflect this truth.

Resources

Richard N. Longenecker, *Galatians*, Word Biblical Commentary (Dallas: Word, 1990).

Scott McKnight, *Galatians*, The NIV Application Commentary (Grand Rapids MI: Zondervan, 1995).

Mark J. Olson, *Galatians: In Defense of Love* (Macon GA: Smyth & Helwys Publishing, 1994).

Klyne R. Snodgrass, "Law in the New Testament," *The Mercer Dictionary of the Bible*, ed. Watson E. Mills et al. (Macon GA: Mercer University Press, 1990).

Steven Westerholm, *Israel's Law and the Church's Faith: Paul and His Recent Interpreters* (Grand Rapids MI: Eerdmans, 1988).

IF GOD GAVE THE LAW, DON'T WE ALL NEED TO OBEY IT?

Galatians 3:1-9, 15-29

Introduction

It's not hard to imagine the conversation of the church business meetings in Galatia. Some Jewish Christians were concerned that this "grace only" doctrine had the potential for unraveling the moral fabric of their society. "The law matters," they would shout. "Surely you aren't suggesting that we can behave however we like without consequences. Remember Sodom and Gomorrah, David and Bathsheba, the exile? There are always consequences. With divine commands come divine punishments. Can't you see where all this grace business will lead?" Persuasive arguments made by charismatic figures bolstered by scriptural references said, "God's going to get you if you ignore the law."

The campaign was very successful in the church of Galatia, and folks were flocking to this "party of the circumcised" whose slogan was "leave the law at your peril." They clearly had the votes in the Galatian church. That's why Paul had to write with such strong language: "You foolish Galatians." Some translate the words with more force: "You idiots" (Philips); "You stupid Galatians" (New English). "Who put a spell on you, bewitched you?" These are the introductory words Paul uses before launching into several skilled arguments dealing with the law.

Before we move to the text and Paul's various points, it is important to be mindful of the context. Paul had a single intent in this letter. He wrote with urgency, as if nothing else mattered. For Paul, this issue was life and death with regard to the future of the Christian movement and the spiritual health of the Galatians. Legalism was a cancer, in Paul's mind, that required radical surgery, so he didn't leave room for ambivalence.

Paul believed a relationship with God is ours for the receiving. We don't have to be worthy of it; in fact, we *can't* be worthy of it. We're sinners, but sin does not make us ineligible for God's love. God's agape love has no connection to merit; it's grace beyond understanding, as demonstrated on the cross. The cross reveals the heart of God, and in it is the nature of the Divine in its clearest revelation. Faith is saying yes to God's gift and trusting that we are loved by the Divine. When we trust in that, we're moving toward being the new creation God intends us to be.

Paul knew the limitations of the law firsthand, so he wrote to folks who wanted to trade in the new gospel for an old legalism. Picture Paul, finally knowing relief and forgiveness, growth and transformation, writing to those who were crawling willingly underneath the huge rock of the law that God had lifted from his shoulders. Picture Paul writing with such concern that his Galatian friends were envisioning a God that demanded moral perfection rather than the gracious God made known in Jesus.

"Are you nuts? Who put a spell on you?" is Paul's explosive beginning. Then Paul accesses his reasoning skills and makes several arguments that you and your class will want to discuss.

I. Remember Your Own Experience

First, Paul makes an appeal to the Galatians' experience. They received the spirit of God before hearing the teaching about circumcision and adopting the Jewish religion. Clearly, the Galatian Christians had an authentic spiritual encounter as they had opened their minds and hearts to the gospel. The Spirit was present to them simply because they opened their hearts and minds to Christ. Paul said, "You got this for free, and now you want to go work for it?" Paul invited the Galatians to be honest about their own experience, to quit dismissing their own story because what they had already experienced with God was valid, and they experienced it by faith.

Too often, we assume the secret to spiritual health lies in some other place, some other authority—the latest book that takes the church by storm—some path or prayer that will change everything. We too easily dismiss our own experience with God in exchange for someone else's truth.

The Galatians had already had an experience with Christ. They were already becoming a new creation. It is so important to learn from others and from the larger tradition, but the Galatians forgot their own experience in the process.

Our relationship to God does not have to be like everyone else's.

II. Remember the Scripture

Paul makes his second argument from Scripture. He uses The Tradition, rather than ignoring it. Abraham was justified by faith. In other words, grace (mercy in the Old Testament) was around long before Moses walked up Sinai and brought down the Ten Commandments. Furthermore, Paul explains, there can be no addendum to a covenant. That's against "covenantal rules" (v. 15). The covenant with Abraham was the first "holy deal" with God. "Abraham believed God," and that was all it took. He was made right with God by his willingness to trust God. So it only follows, Paul contends, that those who place their faith in God are the real sons and daughters of Abraham. Abraham's DNA is not in our bodies, but in our believing.

Those who are trusting in the law alone are in real trouble. Again, Paul plays on the Scriptures. The Old Testament makes it clear that if you're under the law and don't do everything the law says, you're in real trouble, even cursed (v. 10). In verse 22, Paul reminds that Scripture declares that the whole world is a prisoner of sin: "You can look to the law if you like, but you won't get it right...no one has, no one does."

Again, Paul looks within The Tradition for answers. Often, the problem is that we haven't looked deeply enough into our own spiritual home. We haven't appropriated the wisdom available to us in Scripture, so we look to other sources. Paul, however, was a skilled rabbi, and he knew his audience. He recalls for them Habakkuk 2:4: "The righteous will live by their faith."

There is a tendency in the church today to acquiesce to scriptural wisdom too soon. While scriptural wisdom is not the primary emphasis of Galatians 3, we shouldn't miss a chance to learn from Paul. We have a responsibility to engage our churches and the culture as people of biblical faith. With Paul as our model, we can stand against those who would hijack the faith knowingly or perhaps even use the Bible naively.

III. Remember Christ Died for Us

In addition to Paul's adept use of Scripture, he articulates this theology of atonement. While this isn't one of the chosen texts for our study this month, it's important to consider.

Paul gives voice to this understanding of Christ and the cross, which is so prominent in our faith. He begins in verse 1 and then returns to it in verses 13-15. The death of Christ is atoning.

Creatively dividing the word "atonement" has helped many understand its meaning: at-one-ment. Paul's word to the Galatians is that Christ died that we might be *one* with God. Christ's death removed the curse we're under as those who can't live up to the law's demands. Christ has removed this curse so that the blessing given to Abraham—righteousness, right relationship, at-one-ment—can be ours.

This is meat and potatoes for most of us. We know this stuff, and that was Paul's contention with the Galatians. "What is there about this that you don't understand?" Paul is shocked that they seem to have forgotten that Christ's death changed everything.

We should be mindful that believing in atonement with your head and living with a deep sense of at-one-ment with God are often, albeit sadly, two different things. Many who sit in pews and sing this truth are unable to experience it. We can't help ourselves. We crawl back under the law, saying, "I'll get it right this time. I'll just try harder."

God replies, "Was not Christ crucified? What part of forgiven don't you understand?" If you're going to live under the law, then Christ died for nothing.

IV. Remember the Law

Last of all, Paul had to deal with the purpose of the law. So we've come full circle, asking questions that those in Galatia were certainly asking. If grace is the whole deal, then why did God give the law in the first place, and what are we to do with it now? What place does it have? Surely, Paul isn't promoting a kind of immature thinking that asserts, "Morality doesn't matter." Obviously not. Paul's other letters are full of admonitions and guidance about ethical matters, and Jesus clearly expected his follows to "obey his commandments." The law has its place, and in Galatians 3, Paul's explanation for the law is that it points us to Christ.

In the law, we see our sin. We see our inability to live loving, whole lives. We try; we read the commandments, from Moses and Jesus, pull up our moral trousers, and say, "I'm going to do better this time." And maybe we do. But then we feel our chest swelling with pride at our success, and we see again how centered we are in ourselves, how mixed our motives are, even for goodness.

It's exhausting, and Paul would suggest that when that's the case, the law has served its purpose because it's then that we throw ourselves on Christ and honestly say, "Lord, have mercy...I'm a sinner." In this way, the law prepares us for Christ. Although it's not in the text, we should point out that there is a natural progression in most of our lives—a predictability in the pilgrimage. We begin in moral code mode. What's right? What's wrong? What does God require? These are appropriate questions for folks early in the journey. In this stage, a healthy church will offer quick and unquestioned answers, unapologetically.

We all begin at a moral level, just as God's people did. However, it's also necessary that we transcend that level. That doesn't mean, of course, that the law has no place, only that we've come to see it as a means and not an end. It's a spiritual path, and if walked rightly, it can lead us to God's heart. If we worship the path, it leads to death. If any path becomes *the* point, it becomes a dead end.

At the end of this chapter, Paul moves to the important theme: "You are sons of God," presumably with all the rights and privileges, attitudes and actions thereof. Only as we understand our place as beloved children can we appreciate and appropriate the law rightly.

Russian Orthodox Archbishop Anthony Bloom suggests three stages in our relationship to law, three relationships to the Law-giver: slave, servant, son. These stages are not hard to spot in Christians. Slaves obey the law out of fear and resent it. Servants obey out of reward, expecting something in return. But sons and daughters obey out of love (Anthony Bloom, *Living Prayer* [Springfield: Templegate Publishers, 1997] 27).

People who know they are deeply loved, blessed, and accepted view the law with gratitude. They understand it as a gift. They practice the law in hopes of being more loving and becoming more like Jesus. They see the wisdom embedded in it—the wisdom beyond the rules. It's a delight to their eyes, honey to their taste buds, a lamp for their feet, a light for their path, and they hide it deep within their hearts that they might not sin against God.

Notes

Notes

SET FREE
BY CHRIST

Galatians 5:1-6, 13-26

Central Question

What is true Christian freedom?

Scripture

Galatians 5:1-6, 13-26 For freedom Christ has set us free. Stand firm, therefore, and do not submit again to a yoke of slavery. 2 Listen! I, Paul, am telling you that if you let yourselves be circumcised, Christ will be of no benefit to you. 3 Once again I testify to every man who lets himself be circumcised that he is obliged to obey the entire law. 4 You who want to be justified by the law have cut yourselves off from Christ; you have fallen away from grace. 5 For through the Spirit, by faith, we eagerly wait for the hope of righteousness. 6 For in Christ Jesus neither circumcision nor uncircumcision counts for anything; the only thing that counts is faith working through love.... 13 For you were called to freedom, brothers and sisters; only do not use your freedom as an opportunity for self-indulgence, but through love become slaves to one another. 14 For the whole law is summed up in a single commandment, "You shall love your neighbor as yourself." 15 If, however, you bite and devour one another, take care that you are not consumed by one another. 16 Live by the Spirit, I say, and do not gratify the desires of the flesh. 17 For what the flesh desires is opposed to the Spirit, and what the Spirit desires is opposed to the flesh; for these are opposed to each other, to prevent you from doing what you want. 18 But if you are led by the Spirit, you are not subject to the law. 19 Now the works of the flesh are obvious: fornication, impurity, licentiousness, 20 idolatry, sorcery, enmities, strife, jealousy, anger, quarrels, dissensions, factions, 21 envy, drunkenness, carousing, and things like these. I am warning you, as I warned you before: those who do such things will not inherit the kingdom of God. 22 By contrast, the fruit of the Spirit is love, joy, peace, patience, kindness, generosity, faithfulness, 23 gentleness, and self-control. There is no law against such things. 24 And those who belong to Christ Jesus have crucified the flesh with its passions and desires. 25 If we live by the Spirit, let us also be guided by the Spirit. 26 Let us not become conceited, competing against one another, envying one another.

Reflecting

What is freedom? Is there a difference between "freedom" and "license"? If America is the "land of the free," does that mean any behavior must be permitted?

For Christians, the question must drive us back to the Bible, and to the New Testament in particular. In Galatians, Paul examines both freedom and license in detail. His words can guide us in all modern debates about the meaning of "freedom."

Remembering

Last week, we read Galatians 3 and considered the question, "If God gave the law, don't we all need to obey it?" That was surely the question posed by the Judaizers who opposed Paul and who were trying to win the Galatians Christians over to their version of Christianity. After all, Abraham was circumcised, and God told him that all male descendants should be circumcised as well. For more than a thousand years, the Jewish people had continued circumcising their baby boys as a sign of the covenant God made with Abraham. For many it was a simple decision: God gave the law, so we should obey it.

Paul responded to this idea with three arguments designed to demonstrate to Gentile Christians in Galatia that they did not need to obey the letter of Old Testament law. First, he reminded the Galatians that they had already received God's Holy Spirit after coming to faith in Jesus Christ. They received it without obeying the law! Second, God justified Abraham, because of his faith, before he was circumcised. Third, God's covenant with Abraham was based on faith and preceded God's covenant with Moses, which was based on law. All three arguments demonstrate that God is most interested in faith.

Paul knew that his opponents would ask another question: "Why did God give the law if God didn't want us to obey it?" He answered with an analogy about a *paidagogos*, a Greek slave somewhat like a modern nanny. The *paidagogos* taught basic skills such as letters and manners, but when the children were ready for school the *paidagogos* took them to another teacher. His function was temporary. Paul explained that the law also had a temporary function. It was designed to prepare and guide God's people until the Messiah came. But after Christ came, God's people were turned over to him—the master-teacher.

Studying

Paul begins chapter 5 with words that serve both as a conclusion to the previous chapter and an introduction to the theme of "freedom." He begins, "For freedom Christ has set us free. Stand firm, therefore, and do not submit again to a yoke of slavery" (5:1). Apparently, the Galatians were considering the message of the Judaizers carefully, and some were thinking about undergoing circumcision as the Judaizers urged. Paul warned his Gentile readers that such actions minimized the value of what Christ has done. If faith in Christ and his crucifixion is not sufficient, then that faith is not truly a saving faith. God offered grace to all in the death of Christ. That grace is received through faith in Christ. The Galatians were essentially rejecting God's grace if they decided that faith in Christ was not enough for them (2:4).

Second, Paul points out that obeying one part of the law is not enough. In order to be justified through obedience to the law, one has to be "obliged to obey the entire law" (2:3). The Galatians' lives would have been focused entirely on the details of scriptural regulations. Paul understood this kind of life because it is exactly how he lived as a Pharisee before his conversion on the road to Damascus. But Christ came to free people from this kind of obligation. Now that Christ has come, "the only thing that counts is faith working through love" (5:6). The Galatians had to choose between the freedom they already had in Christ and the slavery they would experience under the law.

Apparently, one reason the Judaizers were successful in preaching a legalistic version of Christianity in Galatia is that some of Paul's converts there were falling back into immoral, pagan-type behavior. Some were excusing sinful behavior on the grounds that they were "free" from any kind of behavioral restraints. Paul recognized the problem and attacked it directly—"for you were called to freedom, brothers and sisters, only do not use your freedom as an opportunity for self-indulgence" (5:13). The freedom Christ gives from the law is not freedom from all restraints. Indeed, Christians are free from the law but now are obligated to love one another and act as one another's slaves! Mutual submission is called for.

Paul summarizes his understanding of the law of Moses and Christian moral behavior when he writes, "For the whole law in summed up in a single commandment, 'You shall love your neighbor as yourself' " (5:14). The Greek verb *peplerotai* is translated "summed up" in the NRSV but can also be translated "fulfilled." Paul is saying that Christians do not have to obey every single rule in the Old Testament, but they do *fulfill* the purpose of the Old Testament law when they love their neighbor as themselves.

> In *Israel's Law and the Church's Faith*, Stephen Westerholm shows that Paul is very careful to say that Christians do not "do" the law's commands; rather, they "fulfill" the law (47).

Note that Paul quotes Leviticus 19:18, the same verse Jesus used as the basis for his parable of the Good Samaritan (Lk 10:25-37). According to Jesus and Paul, God's real purpose for the law was fulfilled as Christians demonstrated love for their neighbors.

Unfortunately, the Galatians were not living at all like the Good Samaritan. Instead, they were biting and devouring one another (5:15). They were fulfilling their own individual desires and not showing love for one another. Paul says the Galatians

> And behold, a lawyer stood up to put him to the test, saying, "Teacher, what shall I do to inherit eternal life?" He said to him, "What is written in the law? How do you read?" And he answered, "You shall love the Lord your God with all your heart, and with all your soul, and with all your strength, and with all your mind; and your neighbor as yourself." And he said to him, "You have answered right; do this, and you will live." But he, desiring to justify himself, said to Jesus, "And who is my neighbor?" Jesus replied, "A man was going down from Jerusalem to Jericho, and he fell among robbers, who stripped him and beat him, and departed, leaving him half dead. Now by chance a priest was going down that road; and when he saw him he passed by on the other side. So likewise a Levite, when he came to the place and saw him, passed by on the other side. But a Samaritan, as he journeyed, came to where he was; and when he saw him, he had compassion, and went to him and bound up his wounds, pouring on oil and wine; then he set him on his own beast and brought him to an inn, and took care of him. And the next day he took out two denarii and gave them to the innkeeper, saying, 'Take care of him; and whatever more you spend, I will repay you when I come back.' Which of these three, do you think, proved neighbor to the man who fell among the robbers?" He said, "The one who showed mercy on him." And Jesus said to him, "Go and do likewise." (Lk 10:25-37)

were gratifying "the desires of the flesh" (5:16). Specifically, Paul condemns fifteen behaviors as "works of the flesh"—including "fornication" (sex outside marriage), "sorcery," "enmities" (hatred), "jealousy," "quarrels," and "drunkenness." Paul sternly warns his readers that continuing in this type of behavior will prevent them from inheriting the kingdom of God. This kind of behavior is *not* the freedom that Christ gives.

Paul concludes this chapter by describing life in the Spirit. It is first characterized by love—the Greek word *agape* (5:22). For him, this was the chief characteristic of a Christian lifestyle—all the other virtues he lists arise from a deep love for God and love for others. This love could not be commanded by the law of Moses, but could be created within God's people by the work of the Holy Spirit. Christians are free to experience "love, joy, peace, patience, kindness, generosity, faithfulness, gentleness, and self-control." That is what Christian freedom is all about.

> Every step in the Christian life may be attributed to the work of the Holy Spirit, from conversion (Jn 3:6) to such maturity as reflects "the fruit of the Spirit" (Gal 5:22) (Stagg, 385).

Understanding

Allan Bloom's critique of modern American intellectual society, *The Closing of the American Mind*, begins with this brutal truth: "There is one thing a professor can be absolutely certain of: almost every student entering the university believes, or says he believes, that truth is relative.... Relativism is necessary to openness: and this is the virtue, the only virtue, which all primary education for more than fifty years has dedicated itself to inculcating. Openness—and the relativism that makes it the only plausible stance in the face of various claims to truth and various ways of life and kinds of human beings—is the great insight of our times. The true believer is the real danger" (22).

This stunning insight warns us that young Americans today will not easily accept Paul's claim to specific truth and his condemnation of immoral behavior. Of course, his insistence that Christians are free from the Old Testament law is an easy sell. Who wants to take the time to even read hundreds of regulations from the Old Testament, much less obey them? We are glad to be "free from the law." The Judaizers would make no headway among twenty-first-century Americans!

However, when Paul argues that freedom in Christ does not allow believers to gratify their natural desires, he makes a case not easily accepted by unchurched Americans. Perhaps combining Paul's argument with the words of Jesus himself ensures the best possibility of success. Both Jesus and Paul pointed out that the Pharisees had focused so much on the details of the Old Testament legal regulations that they missed the larger purpose of the law. It was designed to encourage love for God and love for others. Jesus' parable of the Good Samaritan makes that point brilliantly. Paul wants his readers to fulfill exactly that purpose of the law. He wants us to be free of the specific legal regulations, such as circumcision and food laws, but to fulfill the law's purpose by treating one another with love.

Paul steps on all our toes when he lists fifteen specific sins and calls them "works of the flesh." Every one of us tempted toward one of these behaviors should be greatly alarmed by Paul's warning and conclusion that "those who do such things will not inherit the kingdom of God."

More positively, Paul inspires us to allow the love that Christ has planted in us to grow within us the fruit of joy, peace, patience, kindness, generosity, faithfulness, gentleness, and self-control. We love these qualities in others. Everyone enjoys being on the receiving end of such behavior.

How is fulfilling the law's purpose different from fulfilling the law? Which is the higher calling?

What About Me?

• *Attempting to work out a religion based on the Ten Commandments or any law from the Old Testament ultimately devalues the saving work that Jesus Christ did on the cross.* If something more than true faith in Christ is required for salvation, then Christ died for no purpose.

• *Christians are free from the law, but not from all restraint.* Our Christian freedom prohibits us from indulging in many behaviors that feel momentarily appealing. We are still under obligation to love God and to love our neighbors.

• *The Holy Spirit first develops love within the believer, and then the fruit of the Spirit follows, if we simply keep our focus on Christ.* Consider how the Holy Spirit is developing the fruit of the Spirit within you.

Resources

Hans Dieter Betz, *Galatians: A Commentary on Paul's Letter to the Churches in Galatia*, Hermenia (Philadelphia: Fortress, 1979).

Allan Bloom, *The Closing of the American Mind* (New York: Simon & Schuster, 1987).

Richard N. Longenecker, *Galatians*, Word Biblical Commentary (Dallas: Word, 1990).

Mark J. Olson, *Galatians: In Defense of Love* (Macon GA: Smyth & Helwys Publishing, 1994).

Frank Stagg, "Holy Spirit," *The Mercer Dictionary of the Bible*, ed. Watson E. Mills et al. (Macon GA: Mercer University Press, 1990).

Steven Westerholm, *Israel's Law and the Church's Faith: Paul and His Recent Interpreters* (Grand Rapids MI: Eerdmans, 1988).

SET FREE
BY CHRIST

Galatians 5:1-6, 13-26

Introduction

Our home has a certain look to it—a kind of eclectic look. We've got a little bit of everything—some hand-me-downs, some sentimental things that remind us of dear people and places, things we inherited. A few things we've bought for their beauty and a lot for their functionality. A particular style has not been our guide. We mix and match everything...it's our way.

Now imagine that my wife and I are selected as contestants on a reality TV show where a professional redecorates our house free of charge. The only requirement is that we have no choice about how the house is decorated. We are to enjoy a vacation while the decorators work.

So we depart for two weeks in some exotic place and then return to Waco to find our house completely redone. The house is now decorated in a contemporary style—the colors, the furniture, and accent pieces. Everything fits; it's quality stuff, and it's brand new. Modern artwork adorns the walls. It's amazing and wonderful. The decorating team leaves, and we're happy with the new look.

However, in a short while, we start to miss some things: the Norman Rockwell print we received as a wedding gift and the Thomas Kinkade print of a church; that old but very comfortable chair; the desk I built for my wife one Christmas; the tea cart she and her mom bought together years ago. The design team placed all our old stuff in storage, just in case we wanted to give it to our kids for their college apartments. And one day, we just can't resist, so we drive over to the storage closet with the intention of retrieving just a few things, but we wind up with a truckload of the old stuff, and we cram it into our newly decorated home. Our grandparents' old bedroom furniture is right next to a stainless steel lamp. We plop the worn recliner in front of the clean-lined entertainment center. Modern art surrounds Norman Rockwell and Thomas Kinkade.

Well, we like it...we're comfortable again. A few months later the designer returns to check on us, and she's appalled. She, of course, is a purist. You pick a theme and stay with it. You can't mix and match stuff like this without ruining everything. She is beside herself and cannot believe we've messed up something that was so new and wonderful.

I. The Law vs. Grace

The above description is a contemporary picture of what happened in Galatia. The Galatian Christians thought that they could mix and match their "faith home": "We'll take a lot of that new grace and put it everywhere, but we'll also add a touch of 'Early Legalism.' We'll be eclectic and hang a painting of Jesus next to a painting of Moses."

Paul wrote to the Galatians to say, "It doesn't work like that. You can't mix and match Jesus with other things. New wine can't go in old wineskins."

Paul thought in terms of systems: the system of law and the system of grace. In Paul's mind, the two cannot coexist, so he made a very bold statement, saying that if the Galatians chose to be circumcised, Christ was *of no value*. If a person believes that changing his physical anatomy is necessary to gain the blessing of God, that person does not yet understand the gospel. The person isn't convinced that Christ is enough.

Remember that Paul's worldview was one of "principalities and powers" constantly at battle. Legalism and the gospel each demand allegiance, and you can't give allegiance to both. You cannot mix and match these two systems because they are incompatible. So Paul's language is again strong: "If you're trying to be justified by the law, you've fallen away from grace" (v. 4).

What did Paul mean by this statement? Was Paul saying that the Galatians watching their kosher diets and saying their Jewish prayers were no longer accepted by God? Was he saying that they had lost their salvation because of their mistaken thinking? I think not. If eternal security is dependent upon correct thinking, we're all in trouble. How many times have you changed your thinking about God? The Galatians had fallen from grace, but not from God's hand. They were not lost to God, only to themselves and to the transforming experience of grace. God's grace was surrounding them, and they were blocking its effect by decorating their lives with legalism.

In verse 9, Paul uses the yeast in the loaf analogy, reminding his readers that a little yeast goes a long way. In this case, he means that a little legalism goes a long way to creating a person centered in the law. Paul was warning the Galatians that if they allowed a little legalism to creep in, it would influence all of who they were. Grace creates a certain kind of temperament. The same is true with people of the law. An atmosphere of critique tends to follow them. To be sure, at church, they'll express a doctrine of grace, but somewhere behind the closed doors of their soul, they've cut a deal with the legal code, and everything is affected by it. It is not just an idea; it's a force that requires reckoning. "You choose," says Paul. "It's one or the other" (v. 3).

II. The Only Thing that Matters

Now, Paul takes a turn in the epistle. He's stated a hundred ways that we do not need the law to be right with God. Christ is enough. He left no room for the Galatians to misinterpret his meaning: There is no room for the law in the new deal.

Having made that clear, Paul moves to the ethical implication of the gospel, using a phrase that he'll repeat: "Circumcision nor uncircumcision matters." Being religious or irreligious is not the point of the gospel. Some people can make a religion out of being irreligious. Paul has made it clear that getting your religion right doesn't change things with God, but he also warns that being irreligious isn't the answer. Some folks feel the freedom of the grace Christ offers and start to worship their freedom instead of God. It's not hard to imagine Paul's friends strutting about and broadcasting the fact that they weren't narrowed-minded: "We've never been circumcised, and we're proud of it."

The only thing that matters is "faith working itself out in love." "Faith expressing itself through love" is the way J. B. Philips translates it. It is here that we should turn our thoughts to this notion of freedom so prominent in this passage. Paul begins this section by saying that it was for freedom that Christ has saved us. But freedom for what? Freedom to what? What does it mean to be truly free and free in Christ?

Paul answers that question in the latter part of chapter 5: "We're not free in order to indulge our sinful nature." Paul views human beings as possessing two natures: a sinful nature and a spiritual, or "flesh" and "spirit." He believes these two basic natures are constantly at odds with one another (v. 17). Trusting in Christ doesn't remove us from the battle, but it does help us see the nature of it and equip us for the struggle.

Paul understood the depth of the struggle and was careful to say, "Now that the restraint and coercion of the law has been removed, be careful not to indulge your sinful nature." The question arises: What is our motivation for not indulging our sinful nature? Why not give in and let that side have free reign? The answer is obvious, because then we would no longer be free. We would no longer be slaves to the law, but slaves to our own brokenness.

We've been set free in order to manifest our destiny as children of God, as new creations. Christ sets us free to reflect our original innocence—to live out of the image of God, which is our truest and deepest identity. "The fall," life, and our own sin distort that image and the capacity that is ours, but it is still there waiting to be uncovered and freed.

The invitation is to live a life of love—for our faith to work itself out in love (v. 6). Paul uses the remainder of this familiar passage to describe what that is like. If we are centered in the life of the Spirit, we will reflect the qualities of the Spirit. God pours the Spirit into us.

A friend of mine uses the modern metaphor of "downloading" to describe God's action. God's spirit comes into us from above and flows through us into the world. We become conduits of the Spirit. Our task is to remain as free as possible so God's action can take place.

Can we simply choose to be conduits of the Spirit? Paul seems to say yes: "Those who belong to Christ have crucified the sinful nature." I think Paul would tell us that we choose daily, that it involves a million small deaths, rather than one comprehensive dying on our part. We have to keep letting go of, dying to that nature. And that's where the disciplines of the faith come into play...prayer, meditation, service, and fasting just to name a few.

The witness of saints throughout the ages is that once we get hungry enough for the "spiritual fruit" Paul describes, we'll be willing to do the work it takes to grow and become new creations. I hope this doesn't sound like a contradiction of all that's been said so far in this study. It's not. It is, however, an acknowledgement that it takes serious cooperation on our part to be free. We don't pick up freedom in Christ by osmosis, and getting our theology straight about salvation and God's grace doesn't seem to automatically grow good fruit. There are plenty of deacons, Sunday school teachers, and church staff members who are still enslaved to what Paul calls the "flesh."

We're not talking about justification; that question is settled. We're talking about how the justified come to act "justified." We are children of God. How can we live that way? In other words, how can we become what we already are—free? It is for freedom that we've been set free. So let's not give in...not to the yoke of legalism, not to the yoke of our sinful natures. Let's be free indeed.

Notes

Notes

You Raise Me Up

Galatians 6

Central Question

How much responsibility should Christians take for one another's spiritual progress?

Scripture

Galatians 6 My friends, if anyone is detected in a transgression, you who have received the Spirit should restore such a one in a spirit of gentleness. Take care that you yourselves are not tempted. 2 Bear one another's burdens, and in this way you will fulfill the law of Christ. 3 For if those who are nothing think they are something, they deceive themselves. 4 All must test their own work; then that work, rather than their neighbor's work, will become a cause for pride. 5 For all must carry their own loads. 6 Those who are taught the word must share in all good things with their teacher. 7 Do not be deceived; God is not mocked, for you reap whatever you sow. 8 If you sow to your own flesh, you will reap corruption from the flesh; but if you sow to the Spirit, you will reap eternal life from the Spirit. 9 So let us not grow weary in doing what is right, for we will reap at harvest time, if we do not give up. 10 So then, whenever we have an opportunity, let us work for the good of all, and especially for those of the family of faith. 11 See what large letters I make when I am writing in my own hand! 12 It is those who want to make a good showing in the flesh that try to compel you to be circumcised—only that they may not be persecuted for the cross of Christ. 13 Even the circumcised do not themselves obey the law, but they want you to be circumcised so that they may boast about your flesh. 14 May I never boast of anything except the cross of our Lord Jesus Christ, by which the world has been crucified to me, and I to the world. 15 For neither circumcision nor uncircumcision is anything; but a new creation is everything! 16 As for those who will follow this rule—peace be upon them, and mercy, and upon the Israel of God. 17 From now on, let no one make trouble for me; for I carry the marks of Jesus branded on my body. 18 May the grace of our Lord Jesus Christ be with your spirit, brothers and sisters. Amen.

Reflecting

One of the most popular songs at recent graduations has been Josh Groban's "You Raise Me Up." Consider these lyrics for a moment:

> When I am down and, oh my soul, so weary
> When troubles come and my heart burdened be
> Then, I am still and wait here in the silence
> Until you come and sit a while with me.
> You raise me up, so I can stand on mountains.
> You raise me up, to walk on stormy seas.
> I am strong, when I am on your shoulders.
> You raise me up...to more than I can be.

Christians can interpret these words to refer to Christ's help to the believer. Indeed, the line "to walk on stormy seas" seems to be a direct reference to the miracle when Christ walked on the water and saved Peter from drowning. But many students choose this song because it reminds them of teachers, coaches, and even other students who helped them when they were undergoing a difficult time in school. It reminds them of those who helped raise them up when they were burdened by troubles.

In today's session, we'll ask what opportunities Christians have to raise one another up and help one another overcome burdens they face.

Remembering

Last week, we explored the difference between true Christian freedom and the immoral behavior so prevalent in twenty-first-century America. Paul began chapter 5 by pleading with the Galatians not to submit to false teachings. Among the false teachings was the encouragement for males to submit to circumcision. Although Paul had been circumcised as an infant, he believed it would be disastrous for the Gentile Christians to be circumcised. If faith in Christ and his cross was not sufficient to bring full salvation to the Galatians, then what good was the cross? If God's offer of grace through the atoning death of Christ was not sufficient for the Galatians, then they would be rejecting that very grace. Paul was horrified that the Galatians would even consider insulting Christ in this way.

Second, Paul understood exactly what was involved in seeking salvation through works of the law. He pointed out that they would be obligated to obey all the laws in the Old Testament, not simply a select few. Hundreds of regulations would now need to guide their every decision. Paul knew from personal experience that seeking justification in this way was counterproductive. Christ came to free people from this type of obligation.

Third, Paul recognized that some of his converts were falling back into immoral, pagan lifestyles. He lists fifteen specific sinful behaviors in 5:19-21. It is not surprising that Paul's tremendous emphasis on freedom from the Old Testament law had led to some problems. In particular, some Galatians had apparently reverted to their old pagan ways. The Judaizers offered obedience to the laws as a possible solution to the problem of immoral behavior. "If your morals are dropping, adopt the Old Testament law and follow it," they said. Paul countered by challenging the Galatians to "fulfill" the ultimate purpose of the Old Testament law by loving their neighbors as themselves. His statement was reminiscent of Jesus' story of the Good Samaritan. That agape love would also lead to other gifts of the Spirit, which Paul lists. This was Paul's alternative to living a life of obedience to the details of the Old Testament regulations.

Studying

Paul understood that the Galatians were encountering internal problems. Some were sinning openly, and the church members did not know how to deal with this obvious display of sinfulness. Before he concludes this letter, Paul explains what needs to happen when one believer behaves badly: "My friends, if anyone is detected in a transgression, you who have received the Spirit should restore such a one in a spirit of gentleness" (6:1). These words may seem to contradict Paul's own attitude so evident throughout the letter. After all, Paul's verbal blitzkrieg against the Judaizers included two formal curses against them (1:8-9). Who is he to tell us to correct others with "a spirit of gentleness"?! The answer lies in the difference between true heresy and mere transgression. When the basic Christian message of salvation by faith in Christ is threatened, as it was by the Judaizers, then a severe response is required. But when a Christian brother or sister has lapsed into sinful behavior, then Christians must respond gently but firmly.

Giving correction to other believers, however gentle, can easily lead to a feeling of superiority, so Paul warned his readers to watch their own temptations. If they thought they were "something" (meaning "something great"), then they were deceiving themselves (6:3). Jesus warned against the same attitude when he described the Pharisee who prayed, "God, I thank you that I am not like other people—thieves, rogues, adulterers, or even like this tax collector" (Lk 18:11). Clearly, believers exhibiting attitudes like this Pharisee were not fit to restore anyone else from sin. Paul wants to make sure that each person tests his or her own behavior. That behavior is the

"load" that Paul says each Christian must carry for himself or herself (6:5).

Paul describes two additional ways the Galatians could help one another, beyond offering gentle correction to erring brothers and sisters. First, they could share "in all good things" with their Christian teachers—the pastors of their churches. This refers to material support of ministers, such as salary, gifts of food, clothing, or other presents. Just as a farmer who sows generously will reap generously, so will God bless believers who give generously. Paul broadens this point in 6:9-10, calling for Christians to "work for the good of all, and especially for the family of faith." Thus, he called on the members of the Galatian churches to help all fellow believers, not just their pastors. His words, if followed, would lead to congregations who paid their staff well, who helped one another at every opportunity, and who corrected each other with a gentle and humble spirit when necessary. That was Paul's vision for the ideal church.

Apparently, Paul asked his scribe to hand over the pen at this point so he could write the last several verses with his own hand. Paul was forced to write "with large letters" (6:11), possibly because his eyesight was poor or because of some other physical infirmity.

Paul concludes by reiterating his major point about circumcision. His opponents, the Judaizers, wanted to avoid persecution. Most likely, non-Christian Jews were persecuting some of the Judaizers for associating with Gentiles. Paul, in contrast, was willing to face persecution. He followed the example of Christ, who was willing to undergo persecution himself on behalf of others. Because Paul was willing to endure physical suffering, he bore scars from various persecutors. Probably the savage stoning he had received in the Galatian city of Lystra (Acts 14:19) and the 195 lashes he had received at the hands of Jewish persecutors (2 Cor 11:24) had left him scarred for life. He considered those scars "the marks of Jesus branded on my body"

But Jews came there from Antioch and Iconium and won over the crowds. Then they stoned Paul and dragged him out of the city, supposing that he was dead. (Acts 14:19) Five times I have received from the Jews the forty lashes minus one. (2 Cor 11:24)

(6:17). Like his Lord, Jesus Christ, Paul expressed his love for believers by enduring physical suffering on their behalf.

Understanding

Soon after accepting the call to my first church, I read the church's business meeting minutes from the early twentieth century to deepen my understanding of the congregation's history. I was amazed to find that the congregation issued a formal warning to two members for square dancing. If they continued to participate in such dancing, they would lose their membership at the church. Such legalism amazed me, and I thanked God that the congregation was no longer so narrow-minded. Two decades later, I wonder if many of our churches have gone too far in the opposite direction. Do we shy away from even the "gentle correction" that Paul recommends in 6:1?

When one church member leaves his wife and moves in with a girl half his age, do we make any attempt to "restore such a one in a spirit of gentleness"? Or do we simply whisper in amazement about this behavior? What happens in our churches when one man publicly denigrates the church's pastor or when one teenager spreads untrue rumors about a youth minister? Do church leaders attempt restoration or correction when one person uses angry outbursts to intimidate other members? What happens when a businessperson uses church ties to secure a loan from another member but refuses to repay that loan while living a luxurious lifestyle? Today, many congregations are afraid to give even the gentlest correction. Paul's words need to be heard clearly—"if anyone is detected in a transgression, you who have received the Spirit should restore such a one in a spirit of gentleness." Reconciliation must always be the goal and humility the attitude of the ones offering correction. But biblical correction is sometimes needed, and our churches would be stronger if we followed Paul's words more consistently.

Churches would also be stronger if we remembered Paul's promise that we will

Name someone in your church to whom you would gladly say, "You raise me up...to more than I can be." Are there people in your church who think of you when they hear that song?

reap whatever we sow (6:7). We need churches full of people who raise one another up, as Josh Groban's song says. God consistently blesses churches that are full of people who work diligently to bless one another.

What About Me?

• *When we see a fellow church member committing an obvious sin, Paul calls on us to first look within to make sure our attitude is one of humility.* He then calls on us and other church leaders to give gentle correction. Allowing the sin to continue unchallenged may seem like the safer course, but it will weaken our churches in the long run.

• *Most of us can recall people who have made a huge difference in our spiritual lives.* It might be a Sunday school teacher, a football coach, a pastor, or a youth minister who raised us up to be more than we thought we could be. These people "sowed generously," as Paul would say. They worked for the good of other believers and inspired us to achieve more than we thought possible. Paul calls on each of us to be that type of person for someone else in our congregation.

Resources

Ronald Y. K. Fung, *The Epistle to the Galatians*, New International Commentary on the New Testament (Grand Rapids MI: Eerdmans, 1988).

Josh Groban, "You Raise Me Up," *Closer*, lyrics by B. Graham and R. Lovland.

Richard N. Longenecker, *Galatians*, Word Biblical Commentary (Dallas: Word, 1990).

Mark J. Olson, *Galatians: In Defense of Love* (Macon GA: Smyth & Helwys Publishing, 1994).

Steven Westerholm, *Israel's Law and the Church's Faith: Paul and His Recent Interpreters* (Grand Rapids MI: Eerdmans, 1988).

You Raise
Me Up

Galatians 6

Introduction

Alan Cole raises a good question with regard to the last chapter of Galatians. Is Paul speaking generically to all of us, knowing all churches will stumble into sin, or is Paul addressing the specifics of the situation in Galatia (R.A. Cole, "The Epistle of Paul to the Galatians" *Tyndale New Testament Commentaries* [Grand Rapids: Eerdmans, 1978] 170-71)? In other words, when Paul writes of someone "caught in sin," does he imagine someone specific, such as one of the Judaizers? Cole opts for that interpretation. He believes that Galatians is not general pastoral guidance, but an instance where Paul is addressing a particular set of circumstances, as he does in Corinth.

There is no way to know for sure what was in Paul's mind as he wrote, and perhaps it does not matter. In the end, Paul's instructions in this chapter regarding how we are to deal with one another given our sinfulness are helpful and important for all of us. However, as one who is clearly not on the legalistic side of the fence, Cole's thoughts intrigue me.

I. Gentle Restoration

Paul refers to "those who are spiritual," meaning those who are not of the flesh, those who are not obsessed with externals. I like to think that I'm in that group. I suspect some of the Galatian Christians were patting themselves on the back too. It feels good to be in the "spiritual party" and have the Apostle Paul confirm that our way is the right way. In addition, if you have suffered at the hands of the legalists, it feels especially good.

In our elation, we would like to give the legalists, and those who follow them, what's coming to them, confront them in God's name with Paul's teachings, and watch them wiggle. Paul, however, suggests a different way—gentle restoration. If someone is stuck in a sin, restore them gently. Notice that Paul does not say, "If someone sins." No, it's if they are caught, hung up in sin...then go to them in gentleness with restoration as the goal. Paul expects "the spiritual ones" to take the initiative, all the while mindful of themselves and their own weaknesses (v. 1). Paul sees this process as getting under a burden with someone (v. 2), which fulfills the "law" of Christ, a possible play on the word to remind his hearers that they, too, have a law to fulfill. Paul invites them to remember their own limitations (v. 3) as they move into the process of confrontation. Finally, he encourages them not to size themselves up in relation to others (v. 4). Quit the comparison game.

Now, back to Alan Cole's contention that Paul is guiding them as to how to deal with the Judaizers or those who have been led astray by the Judaizers. Clearly, Paul leaves no room for pride, arrogance, anger, or revenge in the process. We go gently, aware of our own stuff and not sizing ourselves up in relation to others.

Accountability and confrontation in a community are touchy subjects. Paul, who had often been the confronter, knew how difficult they were. So Paul anticipated the "call to confront" by those who had been proved right and "of the Spirit" by his letter. He imagined them rallying the "troops of grace" and storming the castle of legalism. Paul cut them off at the confrontational pass: "You who are spiritual, go gently, and go to restore, not to cast out. Go intending to get underneath the burden they are bearing. Watch yourself as you go. Be awake and aware of your own brokenness and your motivation."

Verses 7-10 are an extension of this teaching. Paul commends that as you deal with the one caught in sin, remember that God is ultimately responsible for deciding the consequences: "God's not going to be mocked...folks will reap what they sow." We just need to keep doing good. "Don't grow weary in the process of doing good," regardless of how things appear to be turning out.

So has Paul helped the community avoid dealing with sinful behavior sinfully? Perhaps that was his thinking as he wrote. Perhaps he was afraid the Galatians would take a bad, theologically incorrect situation and make it worse. Historically, it has been true that those oppressed become the next oppressors. Jesus would have none of that. However, should Jesus' followers ignore false teaching and be unconcerned about those caught in sin? The model of Jesus is to intervene. Jesus is God's ultimate intervention.

We don't do much intervening in our churches these days. Why don't we "go to those caught in sin"? Is it our Western individualism? Is it that we haven't earned the right relationally? Is it that we are too afraid or not really concerned about one another? Is it that we aren't sure we fit into the category of "those who are spiritual"?

Perhaps our hesitancy is that we're not sure which sins to confront. Some in our churches could make a quick list of egregious sin. But what about jealousy, envy, discord? Those sins are on the list in chapter 5. Would we confront the preschool teacher for her constant gossip as quickly and as confidentially as the young adult youth worker whose car was at his girlfriend's apartment at 6:00 AM? Would we confront the materialists as well as the alcoholics? Who is going to create the list of sins worthy of the church's confrontation?

II. In Conclusion

Now, Paul has to end his letter. Having encouraged those who are "spiritual" to move toward those who need them, he seems to feel the need to return one last time to his main purpose, which was to warn the Galatians about those among them who would lead them away.

Paul walks the line between gentle, humble confrontation and brutal honesty. He acts as both pastor and prophet. In his previous remarks, Paul has never addressed the Judaizers' motivation. We could simply assume they preached what they did because they were motivated by their convictions.

Paul, however, suggests much less worthy motivations. He accuses them of being motivated by their egos. They are concerned with how they appear (v. 12a). They want statistics (v. 13). Someone at headquarters is going to want a report. They want their monthly bonuses, so they are "compelling" the Galatians to be circumcised. In other words, Paul is saying, "These people don't care about you." They are centered in what is external.

He also says that they are afraid. They preach circumcision to avoid persecution. If you were circumcised, you no longer had to deal with Jewish persecution. What's more, if you were Jewish, the Romans would leave you alone. Judaism was an approved religion, according to the Roman government. Christianity was more threatening to the Romans. So if you were circumcised, you could claim being Jewish when the going got tough. So circumcision was about survival. It was about social viability.

We should be careful about the temptation to be marketable. It is something you hear in church growth circles a good bit. The question is, "What sells?" Now, to be sure, folks are quick to say things like, "It's the same message, just with a new medium," and that certainly can be true. The question is one of motivation and heart. What's it all about—numbers, a pastor's ego, fear that the institution is dying? The ministry of Jesus cannot be carried along by fear or by needy egos.

Paul sees this concern over viability as the real problem. They are afraid and they are small. They need something about which to boast. Paul said that the cross of Christ is the only thing about which he would boast. The world had been crucified to him and he to it. There was no more external need. He had let that go. All that mattered was transformation...a new creation. Paul was not going to boast in his theology of freedom. He was not going to boast in his converts or in his influence in the church. All that mattered was that things were being made new (v. 15).

It is not about circumcision or uncircumcision (v. 15). Neither is the point. It is not about big churches or successful institutions. The point is transformation. It is a simple rule, really (v. 16). And Paul wishes peace and mercy upon all who will follow it.

Notes

Notes

1 Peter
Keep Hope Alive

This study of First Peter focuses on keeping hope alive in the face of pressures and circumstances that could possibly extinguish it completely, or worse, turn authentic faith into a pale replica of the real thing.

Advent Virtues

The phrase "holiday rush" is not an exaggeration. The frantic pace required to purchase gifts, bake holiday foods, and attend Christmas parties, plays, and performances takes its toll; we arrive at Christmas Day exhausted. Within the context of December busyness, the ancient Christian season of Advent takes on new meaning and acquires renewed importance. May God instill the virtues of *hope*, *peace*, *joy*, *love*, and *faith* in each of us this Advent.

Apocalyptic Literature

This study examines five apocalyptic texts in the Bible—from Zechariah, Daniel, Matthew, and Revelation. With each new year bringing a new prediction of impending doom, it is always a perfect time to get the story straight. Apocalyptic literature does not address the future. It addresses our present.

Approaching a Missional Mindset

The World isn't the same as it once was. We must be the church in a new place, in unimagined ways, and with a wider range of people. Engage your small group with the radical and refreshing challenge of developing a "missional lifestyle."

Baptist Freedom
Celebrating Our Baptist Heritage

What makes a Baptist a Baptist? Of course, the ultimate answer is simple: membership in a local Baptist church. But there are all kinds of Baptist churches! What are the spiritual and theological marks of a Baptist? What is the shape and the feel of Baptist Christianity?

The Bible and the Arts

God has used artistic expression throughout the centuries to convey truth, offer blessing, and urge believers to deeper faithfulness. In modern life, artistic expression flourishes, from movies to books to music to paintings to photographs. Sometimes artists are intentional about trying to portray God's truths. Other times, perhaps God is working even when the artist is unaware of it. As believers, we may hear and see God at work in many art forms.

The Birthday of a King

The first four lessons in this unit draw inspiration from a traditional interpretation of the Advent candles as the Prophets' Candle, the Bethlehem Candle, the Shepherds' Candle, and the Angels' Candle. The final lesson, which occurs after Advent, celebrates the theological meaning of Jesus' birth as described in the prologue to John's Gospel.

Challenges of the Christian Life

The way of the cross is difficult, and taking Jesus seriously means looking honestly at how we fall short of God's best hopes for us and seeing how much we need God's grace. For all of us there are times when we need to remember that Christ is our saving grace and recommit ourselves to the journey of faith, rediscovering, again and again, the life-giving purpose described in the book of Ephesians.

Christ Is Born!

Even in the midst of difficult circumstances, Advent is a time when we can find hope. Much like today, people in the 1st century church faced struggles. Examining the Gospel of Matthew, lessons include "Waiting for Christ," "Preparing for Christ," "Expecting Christ," "Announcing Christ," and "The Arrival of Christ."

Christians and Hunger

These sessions challenge us to apply gospel lenses and holy imagination to what literally gives us energy to live: food. With God's grace, we have the opportunity to imagine communities where tables are large and all are fed.

Christians and the Public Square

Politics and faith are tricky areas for Christians to negotiate. The First Amendment to the Constitution guarantees religious freedom for all Americans. As Christians who are also citizens, questions abound: How do we distinguish between faithful and unfaithful forms of civic engagement? How do we give Caesar his due while giving our all to God?

Christmas in Mark

In the early chapters of Mark, we will encounter a Christmas story. This story, however, will not be quite like the one told by other Gospel writers, but it will resonate with the reality of your life. Mark doesn't deny the beauty or reality of the nativity; however, he seems to believe that Christmas begins—the gospel begins—when Christ intrudes upon the hard realities of life.

The Church on a Mission

What does it mean to be a church on a mission? The lesson of Acts 1:8 is that we must simultaneously carry out Christ's mandate at home, in our region, in places that have been our blind spots, and around the world.

Colossians
Living the Faith Faithfully

Paul's letter to the Colossians begins with a high-minded philosophical defense of the faith, but concludes with a collection of extremely practical advice for living by faith. This study addresses the questions many Christians face today, helping them apply Paul's practical advice in their own lives.

Easter Confessions

Easter confession is often found on many different lips in the Gospel of John. When we listen carefully, those ancient confessions still echo into this new millennium.

Embracing the Word of God

We live during a time of transition in Christian history. Basic assumptions about the truth of the Christian faith are being questioned, not only by nonbelievers, but by Christians themselves. First John offers a starting point for understanding of what it means to "be" Christian.

Esther: A Woman of Discretion and Valor

The book of Esther is not a record of historical facts as such. Rather, it is a magnificent narrative that refuses to interpret life as being driven by coincidence or happenstance. In the otherwise unknown characters of Esther, Haman, and Mordecai, we trace the movement of the divine hand as God collaborates with God's risk-taking people to rescue them from the hand of their enemies.

Facing Life's Challenges

This study explores four significant challenges common to most persons of faith: the challenge of new light, the challenge of time's limit, the challenge of living with mystery, and the challenge of authentic spirituality. Although these issues are neither simple nor easy to ponder, this study effectively leads us in confronting these challenges.

Forgiveness and Reconciliation

Forgiveness is a central issue in our capacity to remain redemptively connected to those relationships we prize. Restoring broken or interrupted relationships is a primary issue for all of us, and managing forgiveness is crucial to the possibility of experiencing reconciliation. Several dimensions of forgiveness affect our lives in significant ways. In this study, we attempt to address a few of those important issues.

The Four Cardinal Virtues

Christians are learning how to distinguish between members of a church and disciples of Christ. Discipleship involves developing virtues in those who come to our churches seeking life, salvation, grace, mercy. If we want to have something to offer a world in desperate need, then we must return to virtues like discernment, justice, courage, and moderation. We must return to the hard and glorious work of making disciples.

Galatians
Freedom in Christ
Paul wrote with fiery passion, as you will notice from the opening paragraphs of this letter to the Galatians. But his language reveals that he was writing about a crucially important issue—the very nature of salvation in Christ.

Godly Leadership
Nehemiah was called to return to Jerusalem to lead in the sacred task of rebuilding the city's walls. Displaying characteristics often lacking in secular leadership—prayerful humility, a willingness to work with diverse teams, wisdom in confronting conflict, and a passion to stand with the powerless—Nehemiah offered his people a portrait of godly leadership that can still shape our own calls to lead nearly 2,500 years later.

A Holy and Surprising Birth
Christmas begins here—discover these five love stories from the book of Luke and renew your appreciation of God's laborious effort to birth our salvation.

How Does the Church Decide?
An array of decisions draw energy and time from church members. These decisions may be theological, such as mode of baptism, aesthetic, such as the color of the sanctuary carpet, or functional, such as the selection of a new minister. This study will consider how the church has made its decisions in the past to help guide our decisions today.

Is God Calling?
Witness the varying forms of God's call, the variety of people called, and the variety of responses. Perhaps God's call to you will become clearer.

James
Gaining True Wisdom
If we'll be honest with God and ourselves as we study what James says, we can make great strides toward wisdom and a living faith.

Life Lessons from Bathsheba
Who was Bathsheba? She was a complex figure who developed from the silent object of David's lust into a powerful, vocal, and influential queen mother.

Life Lessons from David
In the Bible, we catch David in the various stages of the human journey: childhood, adolescence, adulthood, and senior adulthood. From the biblical treatment of the stages of David's life, we can land some insights to assist us in better understanding the human journey.

The Matriarchs
The matriarchs of Genesis offer their lives as a testimony of faith, perseverance, and audacity. We learn from their mistakes and suffering. We will gain the hope of Hagar, the joy of Sarah, and the audacity of Rebekah as we are challenged to examine our prejudices and our insecurities while studying Esau and Jacob's wives.

Missional Hospitality
If we are serious about following Jesus, we will be people of open hearts, open hands, and open homes. In other words, as followers of Jesus we will practice the fine art of hospitality. In lesson one, we reflect on hospitality to strangers. In lesson two, we address hospitality to the poor. In lesson three, we focus on hospitality to sinners. In lesson four, we learn about hospitality to newcomers. Lesson five reminds us about our hospitality to Christ.

Moses
From the Burning Bush to the Promised Land
We would do well to trace the life of Moses so we might discover how his life changed, both personally and as Israel's leader, as he learned what it meant to love God with all his heart, soul, and strength.

Old Testament Promises to God

Some individuals may feel that our promises couldn't possibly mean anything to God. Perhaps the real question is this: under what circumstances should or do we make such promises? The Old Testament contains several examples of people making promises to God, using the unique form of a biblical "vow."

The Passion of Christ

The four lessons in this unit highlight the faith struggles of the early disciples. In lesson one, Jesus addresses the issues of faith and practice. In lesson two, we meet Judas who, like us, struggled with God's Kingdom and human kingdoms. In lesson three, the issue of temptation reminds us that our faith journey is a constant challenge. Lesson Four invites us to remember Peter's experience of "faith failure." Peter's failure, however, is not the final word. There is forgiveness.

The Prayer Life of Jesus

The study of Jesus' prayer life can deepen our own prayer practices. These five sessions examine the importance of prayer at various stages of Jesus' life and ministry. He made no important decisions without consulting God.

Prepare the Way

In these sessions, we will seek to prepare the way toward and into the Christmas season. We begin with the theme of hopeful watchfulness in light of the coming of Christ. Next, we will spend two sessions considering the ministry of John the Baptist, the forerunner of Christ. Then, we will consider Matthew's account of the birth of Jesus and join in wonder at the miracle of "God with us." Finally, we will remember the story of the "holy innocents" killed by Herod in his attempt to eliminate the Christ child's threat to his power.

Proverbs for Living

Long ago, a collection of wise teachers committed themselves to the ways of God and collected this wisdom into what we know as the book of Proverbs. These four lessons explore the simple truth of Proverbs: there is a good life to be had—a life lived in faithfulness to God.

Qualities of Our Missional God

Too often we are tempted to let "numbers" drive missions. The book of Numbers reminds us that missions is motivated by something deeper. Missions reflects the heart and nature of God. If we can just get past the math, we can see God's nature clearly in the book of Numbers. . . in the wilderness.

Responding to the Resurrection

All major events of human history elicit responses as varied as the personalities and situations represented by those affected. No one witnesses a world-changing event without being affected in some way. Studying the response of early followers helps us to shape our own response to the resurrection of Jesus. Each of us must consider our response to Jesus' life, teachings, death, resurrection, and call on our lives.

The Seven Deadly Sins

What exactly is sin? Just as we organize our cupboards and our schedules to make sense of our lives, Christian thinkers have organized sin into a number of categories in order to understand and surrender these patterns to God. The notion of "seven deadly sins" emerged as a way to recognize specific dangers to our spiritual lives. The purpose of the book is to guide people away from sin and into a wise and godly life.

Seeking Holiness in the Sermon on the Mount

The Sermon on the Mount has long been recognized as the pinnacle of Jesus' teaching. But with this importance in mind, it's easy to think of Jesus' teachings as lofty and idealistic, offering little guidance for everyday life. Perhaps Jesus' sermon allows us to see beyond ourselves, beyond our own failures and shortcomings—revealing God's intention for our lives.

Sing We Now of Christmas

In this study, we will explore some familiar prophecies, as well as the Gospel birth narratives, through the lens of five traditional Christmas carols. As carols have grown to be a fuller and more meaningful part of our worship and celebration, so too can the stories of Jesus' birth continue to grow within us and enrich our faith experience.

Spiritual Disciplines
Obligation or Opportunity?

The spiritual disciplines help deepen a believer's faith and increases his or her intimacy with Christ. In this study, we take a deeper look at some of the disciplines and consider their practice as a response to God's love.

Stewardship
A Way of Living

Great News! Stewardship is not about money! At least not *just* about money. Certainly, stewardship relates to money, and, yes, we need to tithe. However, stewardship branches out into multiple areas of life. Properly practiced, this act of service can lead to peace and purpose in living.

The Ten Commandments

When the Ten Commandments are in the news, it is usually because a judge or teacher has hung them up on the walls. The Ten Commandments do not need to be posted or even preached nearly so much as they need to be practiced and viewed as life-giving, joyful affirmations of a better way of life.

War, Peace, and the Bible

As people of faith, we are faced daily with an expectation that we participate in violent actions, our willingness to allow violence in the world to continue, and our response to violence in our lives. Is there a place for war and violence in our faith?

What Would Jesus Say?
A Lenten Study

To address what Jesus would say, we need to discover what Jesus did say. These lessons will attempt to help us understand Jesus' teachings and apply them today.

The Wonder of Easter

In 1 Corinthians 15, Paul asserts that the message that Jesus died for our sins, was buried, and rose on the third day is "of first impor-tance" (v. 3). It is the core of the gospel story and of the Christian faith. But as much as Easter is a mystery to contemplate, it is also a hope to embrace and good news to proclaim.

**NextSunday Studies
are available from**

Made in the USA
Middletown, DE
22 February 2023